Arnout Verzijl & Hans Willink

BARNEY

The Eye of the Tiger

The authorised biography of a Dutch dart playing legend

STRENGHOLT
UNITED MEDIA

Colophon

Authors	Arnout Verzijl & Hans Willink
Title	Barney: the eye of the tiger. The authorised biography of a Dutch dart playing legend
Photography	Hans Willink & Raymond van Barneveld's own archives, unless stated otherwise. Although we did our utter best to retrieve the rights of the photo on page 4, we did not succeed. Anyone claimiing to have a right to this picture can contact the publisher.
Translation	Mercury Translations Ltd., London, United Kingdom
Design	De Ontwerpunie, Huizen, The Netherlands
Printing	FINIDR s.r.o., Český Těšín, Czechia
ISBN	978 90 4940 051 4
NUR	491: sport, biography

Strengholt United Media BV
Hofstede Oud-Bussem
Flevolaan 41, 1411 KN Naarden
Postbus 338, 1400 AH Bussum
T: +31 (0)35 69 58 430
F: +31 (0)35 69 58 440
E-mail: unitedmedia@strengholt.nl
www.strengholt.nl

Contents

WHYTE & MACKAY
BARRY LEECH
PLANT HIRE
unicorn

Foreword

When I was asked to write the foreword for Barney's book, I immediately said yes. Barney is without doubt one of the best players ever to stand on the oche.

The first time we met was during the European Championship in Malta in 1990, although at that time we did not really know each other and it was to be some years later that we became more acquainted. Due to the break-away and the formation of the PDC, we didn't really get to play each other back then, and we both went ahead over the next few years and became very successful in our respective organizations.

The first time we really talked was in the preparation of our first TV-battle at Wembley in 1999. I beat him, but I knew he was the challenge for the future. And I was right, because after 1998 and 1999, he won the Lakeside also in 2003 and 2005.

My respect for Raymond is enormous. He is very professional, has a good sense of humor and is a winner. He can't stand losing and that is exactly the reason he is 5-times World Champion.

When he came over to the PDC, there were a lot of people saying maybe he would not be able to cope with the travelling and extra competition. I knew that he would be one of the big challengers, and would be someone that would make me have to work harder to stay at the top.

He certainly announced himself in style by hitting a 9 darter live on TV during his Premier League match against Peter Manley. His first year culminated in that thrilling World Championship final against me, when it seemed like the whole world had watched!

His switch to the PDC was the best decision he could make, and the final we played in 2007 is without doubt a major reason why darts has continued to grow all around the world.

I think the story about Raymond written in this book will explain why he is the player and person he is now. The quiet, maybe even shy guy from The Hague who is a ruthless winner on stage.

Phil Taylor

The postman delivered

When you consider that he used to deliver the post, the fact that Raymond van Barneveld started receiving letters and messages from the Queen reinforces that the last decade has been quite remarkable for the The Hague born darts star of The Netherlands.

The day after Raymond won his first BDO World darts title Schiphol airport was besieged. Alongside air traffic control it was crowd control that was needed, thousands turned up to cheer their Dutch world champion. In many people's eyes it was a turning point, not just for Raymond, but for the sport of darts. The Dutch influence on the sport in recent years has been immense, Frimley Green Surrey turns into a suburb of Amsterdam every January, new young Dutch darters emerge, all wanting to be the new 'Barney'.

This book charts the story of the postman who became a national sporting hero, it will reveal the many twists and turns there were along the way. Making such a journey is never straightforward and the world of darts isn't without major rivalries and rows many of which are chronicled in the pages to come.

Having witnessed at first hand Raymond's dedication and determination, having seen at close quarters his elation when he wins and the desolation he feels in the immediate aftermath of defeat the story of his assent to the top of his sport, and how he crossed codes to add the PDC world title to the BDO world title is a fascinating read.

We all have phrases and sayings we go by in life. 'Speak as you find', is one that works for me. I have always found Raymond warm and friendly, but fiercely competitive, you don't get to be world champion by being a soft touch.

The postman that delivered the world championship to his fans and inspired an entire nation. Quite a story.

Ray Stubbs

Presenter BBC Television

Introduction

RAYMOND VAN BARNEVELD is a one off, unique. Each time he competes in a thrilling darts final, millions of people stay glued to their television screens, watching this Dutch guy from The Hague perform. In 1995, he made it to the final of *The Embassy* for the first time. This legendary darts tournament is held every year in the English village of Frimley Green. Just three years later, in January 1998, he became the first non-English speaking player ever to win the competition!

Through the ensuing years, Raymond has become an international sporting legend. His fellow countrymen united in pride and reflected glory with each passing success. However at other times, certainly in the early days, he has also been loathed by them. At times, with their hopes dashed by under-achievement, nothing is more typical of the Dutch than to put down their home-grown hero in his time of need. The British however seem to have reacted differently to the highs and lows of Raymond's darting career. Even though Van Barneveld is Dutch, he is consistently highly regarded on the other side of the North Sea, whatever his results.

The reason for this difference in attitude may stem from more than just another country's way of thinking. It is sheer respect for Raymond van Barneveld's massive achievement of single-handedly relieving the proud English peoples of one of their traditional sporting crowns. As there is nothing more quintessentially British than to go to the pub after work or at weekends to relax, have a beer or two, play some darts and enjoy quality time among friends.

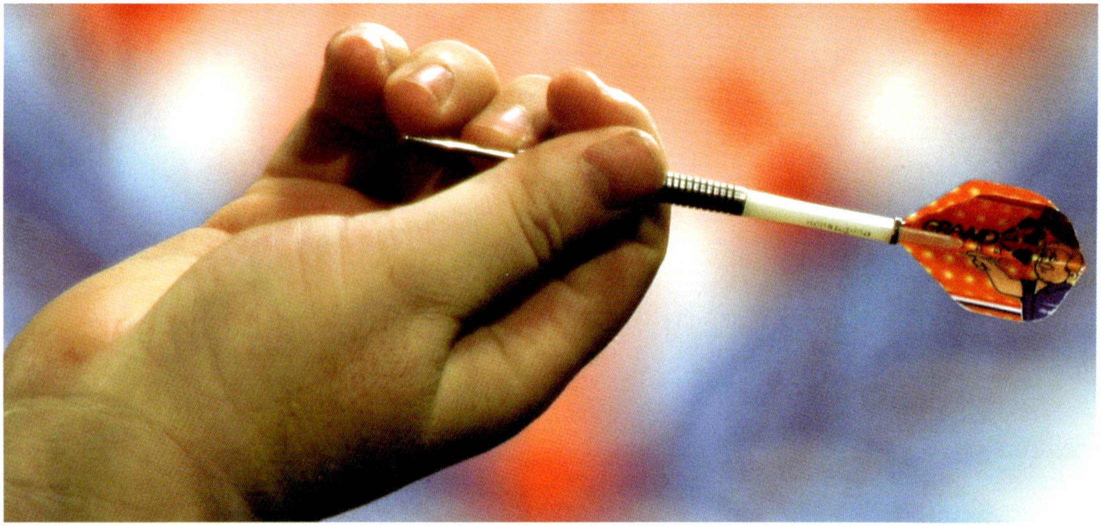

During the final decades of the 20th century darts grew exponentially, becoming an extremely popular pub game. Many new national competitions were established, promoted and some even televised. Mean while many additional umbrella darts associations were founded and flourished. Yet the basic character of darts remained primitive and primarily a game for amateurs, heading into the 80's. The Dutch were first able to view the game when BBC TV started to be relayed and transmitted to the population of the west coast of The Netherlands. It was then, during the eighties that they were offered their first taste of a major darts competition: *The Embassy*.

Raymond thinks that his popularity and fame stem primarily from his impressive displays of dart playing at this tournament. *The Embassy*, renamed Lakeside in 2004 – and now named in full, Lakeside World Professional Darts Championship, is an official world professional championship darts competition organised by the British Darts Organisation (BDO).

Right from the start in 1991, during his first tournament, the British embraced 'The Postman from The Hague' with open arms. He had no immediate success there that year but the darts fans still quickly nicknamed him Barney after the cartoon figure from the television series The Flintstones. Not knowing that during his school days in The Netherlands his nickname was the same.

In the 80's and 90's, there was still no real money to be made by dart players and in The Netherlands, the sport was still in its infancy.

Only the very best English players could survive and continually make a living as professionals.

When the members of the BDO established *The Embassy* tournament in 1978, it was the first big world darts championship to be developed. The tournament, spanning two weekends and the week between, provided some spectacular sporting entertainment. It was given a lot of TV airtime and also offered excellent prize money.

The window of opportunity was just over one week, once a year, to conjure up a performance of the highest order. That was all Van Barneveld had and he was very much aware of the fact. He managed this by being able to convert the stress, strains and emotions of a lonely childhood into an unprecedented drive for victory.

His UK victories started a chain reaction in The Netherlands, as darts took off, big time. The BDO also benefited from his success. He was an international player, with a level of professionalism unknown at the time to the British. In The Netherlands many great tournaments were initiated as follow-ons. By 2006, Raymond had already won four Lakeside titles. This was the year that he made up his mind to make yet another bold career move. He left his comfort zone of the BDO and joined their rival, the Professional Darts Corporation (PDC). Why, because he wanted to become the very best dart player in the world.

In spite of all his success Raymond has always remained down to earth, acting much the same way as he did when he was a postman. Shy, not too confident and always searching for recognition.

Vincent van
datadart
RAYMOND

Three key moments

Monday afternoon January 14th 1991

Raymond van Barneveld had completely had it. Sitting on the boat, plying its way from Harwich to the Hook of Holland, he was still searching for answers. He couldn't understand it: "why?" That was the question going through his head continually. The experience of his defeat in England was slowly ebbing but he remained completely down and out. He was managing somewhat to fight off the pain of a swift defeat in the first round but was still overwhelmed by an intangible feeling of guilt. He went for a walk, out on the deck. Noticing the heavy grey clouds clustered together, hanging above the North Sea, he thought "just how am I going to explain to everyone?" Down-heartedly and worried he stared at the rolling grey-blue waves.

Raymond van Barneveld had lost the remainder of his fragile confidence: His very first Embassy and he was knocked-out in the first round! The wildcard invitation he had been granted by the BDO for entry into this world-famous tournament, had been viewed by others with some scepticism all along. So going out in the first round quickly turned the dream into a complete nightmare. He not only disappointed himself, but others too. Financially Van Barneveld was going through a tough time, depending on other peoples' generosity to support him. These were well-meaning people who had backed the twenty-something from The Hague to become an over night sensation. He had let them down he thought, as he had the dart loving public of The Netherlands. Everybody back home thought that he was already capable of winning *The Embassy*. After all he was now the most talented darts player in Holland.

Of course the English darts elite barely took much notice of him during the tournament. Holland? To them, that was nothing more than a third world darts country. Dutch dart players were thought of as cannon fodder at the time, tournament fillers, crowd pleasers. Van Barneveld had felt the disregard in the air and it had troubled him.

Since the initiation of an, at the time, un-official Darts World Championship in 1978, the game had been controlled by the UK competitors. '*The Embassy*' was the annual showpiece of the organising BDO. Now the word on the street was that Van Barneveld would become the first foreigner to break this traditional supremacy.

But that was not the case and proved unrealistic. Breaking UK supremacy of a historically and unique sport such as darts, was proving to be a distant utopia, even at the beginning of the 90's. As the then unknown Australian Keith Sullivan ended the dreams of the then 23-year-old Dutchman 3 sets to 0.

Reality was harsh: Raymond could now only fall back on a job in the building industry, as a carpenter. Or perhaps as a postman. Making it as a darts player, winning international tournaments and earning a living as a pro? No way now! On that boat ferrying between England and Holland those ambitious and thoughts were quickly jettisoned.

Shaking his head in disbelief he slowly went back inside and down the stairway to a lower deck. His face was already reflecting the highly self-critical torment that would continue haunting him on the trip home across the North Sea.

Sunday evening January 11th 1998

The atmosphere at the Lakeside Country Club was hard to describe. Tense was not a strong enough expression. Electrically charged or even explosive would have been more descriptive. The fanfare leading up to the final was really high-powered. When, after few more minutes the sound of booming rock music died down, the master of ceremonies Martin Fitzmaurice called both finalists up on to the stage. Their rest was over.

Richie Burnett, a determined look on his face, stepped onto the boards. This outstanding dart player with the nickname, *'The Prince of Wales'* had already lost a final before and showed no intention of repeating the experience. Two years earlier, he had lost to Steve Beaton 6 sets to 3. He probably preferred to cast his mind back to the 1995 Championship. In this final he beat the new pretender Raymond van Barneveld who had, surprisingly made it to the final, also by 6 sets to 3. As this time, the slightly older neighbouring countryman was his opponent again!

While about a hundred-odd fans dressed up in orange were screaming at the top of their voices, both the matador and the aspiring banderillo fired their series of practise darts at the board. For only the second time in the history of the most important darts competition in the world, a Dutch player was throwing in the final. Raymond was out for revenge. This time the title was going to be his! He knew no one could stop him now. Not even someone answering to the name of Burnett from the Rhondda.

At the half way stage the score was 3-2 to Barney but overall each player was not giving the other any leeway. The deafening, diehard UK audience was backing their fellow countryman to the hilt. This had the effect of throwing petrol onto a fire to the highly competitive Dutch underdog. Raymond van Barneveld has already cleverly learnt to ignite his motivation using his setbacks in any shape or form as the tinder. In the run-up to this '98 Embassy one of his major sponsors withdrew at the very last moment, almost ruining his chances of finally kick starting an eagerly awaited professional career but he managed to soldier on.

Focused and methodically Van Barneveld kept throwing his arrows. Consistently they landed clustered together in the holy of holies spot, the triple 20. Outwardly he looked apparently undisturbed but inwardly he was on fire with passion and desire.

However, the persevering Welshman Burnett, slowly drew level on sets and then pulled clear by winning the seventh, seemingly well on the way to victory now.

Not so, Van Barneveld fights back to level it again at 4-4 and wins the ninth convincingly 3 legs to 0. He led 5-4 on sets and now was just one set away from a sensational and historic victory.

His opponent steeled himself once more, shrewdly roaring at the audience, evoking the required response and managed to squeeze out an energy-consuming late offensive. It was now 5 sets all and so a 11th and final, decisive set was needed to determine who would win.

The Country Club was bursting to the seams with excitement. The audience was ecstatic. The alchemic mix of the unique situation was being stirred in with the passion of all the fans. The final approached an unprecedented climax. Both players still managed to hold their nerve. The first four legs of the final set were shared equally. 2-2. Then, as it was the last set, a tiebreak was called. The eventual winner needing a difference of two legs advantage over the other.

They moved cautiously into the fifth leg. Here, at this stage, Van Barneveld finally managed to break Burnett, who also had the advantage of throwing first. It was now 3-2. Carrying this momentum on, the Dutchman now seemed to be more composed, as he threw first for the sixth leg of the final set.

The leg took shape and was going Barney's way. After several more throws he needed just a double 8 to finish and win. Time seemed to stand still. He took aim and threw the dart carefully to the left of the board. Spinning gracefully, it nestled itself firmly into the 8 mm wide red double track-ring of the 8 sector on the African Sisal BDO approved Winmau, as if it was coming home. Result!

Van Barneveld fell to his knees clasping his face in his hands. Then cried out at the top of his voice in elation, his last dart of the tournament thrown immaculately.

As he shed his tears of happiness in England, in The Netherlands hundreds of thousands of Dutch TV viewers watching the championship at home jumped for joy, sharing his personal and national pride at succeeding against all the odds.

Van Barneveld was crowned the first foreign champion of a bastion of British indoor sport, darts. Yes, the Brits had been defeated at their own game, at their own specialty. For a while, Van Barneveld became one of the happiest men alive. His life had changed forever.

Monday evening January 1st 2007

The boisterous audience in the compact Circus Tavern situated in the English town of Purfleet knew it was in for a grand finale, a dream darts final. The PDC World Championship was being contested by the two best darts players in the world: Raymond van Barneveld and Phil (The Power) Taylor. The Brit seemed to be struggling, or was he? Continually he lost his advantage during the match. Raymond's fighting spirit however seemed to lift the Dutchman's performance.

Van Barneveld had built a reputation of coming off best when involved in close, exciting duels. Often, very often he had won a game based on his unassuming competitive spirit pulling him through. Classed as the underdog, he had fought back numerous times in the past to this end. But could he do it again, facing thirteen-fold world champion Phil Taylor?

Up until that moment, Taylor had been, unequivocally and unquestionably the best darts player in the world. The Brit from Stoke-on-Trent won his first Embassy way back in 1990. In 1992 he repeated that victory. Then out of the blue a year later, Taylor contributed his part to the Great Divide that split the darts world in two. The break was stimulated by the lack of initiative by the BDO to lobby for more TV coverage of the game and sponsors. Phil, together with nearly all of the greatest dart players in the world, left the BDO and created another organisation, originally named the World Darts Council. This organisation is nowadays recognised as the Professional Darts Corporation (PDC).

The mass exodus from the BDO of course cleared the way, giving young up and coming talent a chance to make a name for themselves. As a consequence the Canadian John Part became the first non-British player to win *The Embassy* in 1994. A year later Van Barneveld stormed through the competition but he was beaten by Burnett in the final.

Right from the word go of the formation of the PDC, excepting the difficult start-up phase, Taylor had reigned supreme. The first World Championship of this new league took place without his presence. However, he won the following eleven titles in a row to make up for it! Through the years Taylor became *The King* of the PDC. Arguably holding the status of being the best darts player that the world had ever seen. This may well have been the overriding reason for Raymond deciding to transfer from the BDO to the PDC in 2006. The wish to emulate Taylor, by beating him.

It had taken years for Van Barneveld to accept the supremacy of his opponent. Only after he managed to achieve this was his critical mind relaxed enough to consciously want to seek out regular darting duels with Taylor.

Van Barneveld was challenged to call on all his experience, gained over the 20 years of his darts career, on that fantastic and historic New Year's Day event in 2007. The neck and neck duel between these two titans was building up the excitement set-by-set. It kept the Brits, Dutch and millions of other darts fans all over the world, glued to their television screens. Now tied 6-6 on sets and 5-5 on legs. "Sudden Death 501" was hoarsely called. They played a dart each fired at the bull, to decide who began. The tension was almost tangible.

Van Barneveld started cautiously then Taylor showed his class immediately by opening with 180. Calmly he imprinted his quality on the board. Or so it seemed.

Van Barneveld remained collected and responded by matching Taylor with another max score of… "A hundred and eighty". 13 times world champion Taylor was visibly taken aback.

At 40/90, 13 darts later, Van Barneveld took hold of the PDC 2007 world title by bedding the last dart of the competition in the double top! Now he was a 5 times world champion, equalling Eric Bristow's achievement. His euphoria on winning rose to equal that of the audience. Van Barneveld's English fans *The Barney Army* began chanting his nickname continuously, Barney! Barney! Long in to the night.

Taylor had been well and truly beaten on the night and dethroned. He had stumbled on his second throw, recovered then stumbled again in sight of victory on his fourth.

Van Barneveld searched for his wife Silvia in the audience. Forgotten were all the difficult times in his life. Gone was his fear of failure and lack of confidence. Vanished, the thought: "what now you good for nothing?" He had finally been able to extinguish his continual self-doubt about his performances.

For a split second, the world seemed to be spinning around him and him alone, as the darts world hailed its new king. "Long live the King."

The darts world hails a new king. Raymond van Barneveld has beaten Taylor to win the PDC world title.

Wesselstraat, Transvaal, The Hague

Raymond van Barneveld was born in Transvaal, a working class neighbourhood, southwest of The Hague in The Netherlands. He was not the only famous Dutchman to be born or live in this area of The Hague. Wim Deetman, Mayor of The Hague from 1996 to 2007, was also born there. The neighbourhood was part of continual residential development between two world wars, spreading southwards towards Kijkduin. The houses in the area were mainly constructed between 1930 and 1935 together with the Haagse Markt, The Hague Market. Nicknamed locally "De Maag" or "The Stomach" in English.

An open-air market located on the Herman Costerstraat, now regularly supporting 500 stands and has about 40,000 visitors each market-day. Said to be the largest day market in The Netherlands and also in Europe.

Raymond considers his years growing up in Transvaal to be the happiest period of his youth. There was always something to do and enjoy. Just strolling around the Haagse Markt or helping the market traders to clean up. Games, collecting discarded Christmas trees for bonfires or playing football and other games.

The Van Barneveld family was not well off. Raymond's dad, Rob earned a reasonable living as a carpenter and brought in a modest pay packet most weeks. Thanks to the system of holiday coupons, allowing construction workers who changed employers regularly to save for holidays, Raymond was even able to go with his family once on a trip abroad during his childhood. Life was not too bad he thought at the time... but if only the house they lived in was a bit bigger.

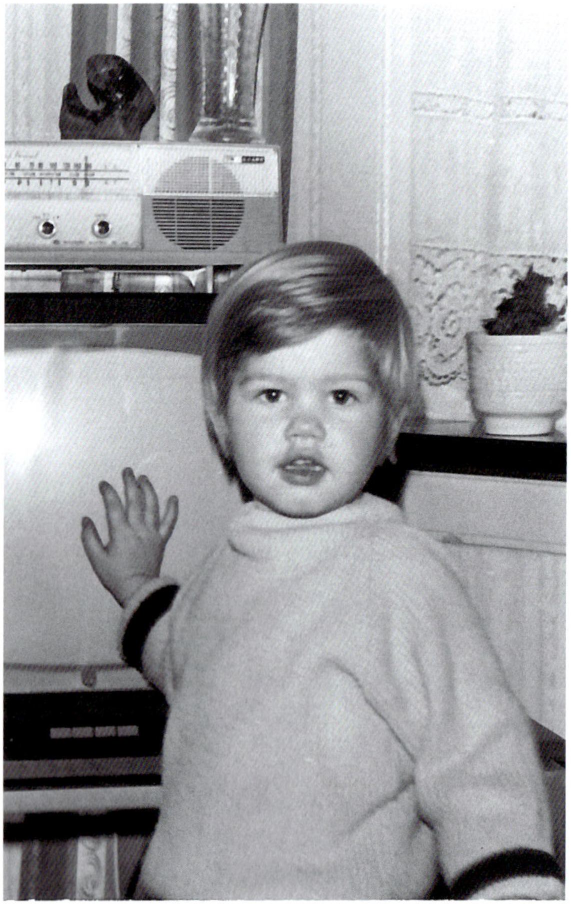

The happiest period of Raymond's childhood was growing up on the Wesselstraat in Transvaal, The Hague where he lived until he was 9.

Raymond: "I was born on the 20th of April 1967 and grew up on the Wesselstraat right next to the Haagse Markt situated on the Herman Costerstraat. I had a lot of friends there, both boys and girls. We were always playing outside; our neighbourhood was really made for it. We played football, marbles and sometimes of course played a few tricks here and there. That was all part of the fun. At the end of each day we used to help the merchants close-up their market stalls. We went there a lot because there was always something to do around the Herman Costerstraat. For example if we happened to find a few of rotten tomatoes or oranges, we would try to hit the side of the passing trams with them. I was a bit of a rascal in those days, I guess.

My primary school, the Prinses Beatrixschool, was situated on the Fischerstraat, very close to the Wesselstraat. All the kids at school lived in the neighbourhood. We were a tightly knit group, everybody knew everybody else. We loved being mischievous. Our favourite pastime was playing 'kerbing', we loved it. It's a game where you had the throw a ball at the kerb across the street. Traffic was no problem at the time as there were far fewer cars on the streets. But when a car did park up, we always felt it seemed to happen right where we were playing, while there was still loads of room for it to park further down the street. Sometimes we also walked along to the Kaapseplein but no further, that was it really. Our neighbourhood has changed a lot now. It was not multicultural in those days. If fact we did not even know what the word meant back then.

A class picture taken at the Prinses Beatrixschool. Raymond is wearing a beige turtleneck jumper and looking at the photo standing fourth from the right on the 3rd row from the front. Raymond had some happy times there.

An annual highlight at the time was the Christmas tree fight, in which the Wesselstraat competed against the Fischerstraat and the Herman Costerstraat. We used blowpipes as weapons and paper arrows as the ammo. Of course we put needles in the tips; otherwise it wouldn't have hurt, as that was our intention. There would be thirty or forty of us fighting each other like crazy. The bigger boys were in command and the small ones like me, just went along with the mayhem. The big boys would go and watch the top local football team, ADO Den Haag, play nearby. Consequently, we admired them endlessly. The Zuiderpark football stadium was only two blocks away from where we lived but still forbidden territory for me. There was simply not enough money for a ticket. Entry cost maybe only five guilders, but the family still could not spare that kind of money in those days. Many times I used to confide in my mother: 'When I grow up mum, I want to be rich.' I have no real idea where I got the notion from, but I always used to repeat this over and over again to her.

His mother, Anneke van Barneveld has a big heart. Digging back into her memory she mentioned: "Raymond and I liked to listen to music together, especially guitar music. Bands like Foreigner and Queen. We both enjoyed that. We also watched Dutch TV's AVRO's Top Pop and Benny Hill, together with Barney's friend Dick Pronk. Benny Hill made us laugh a lot at the time.

When he used to come home in the afternoon, I often sent him upstairs. Otherwise he would just lie down in front of the stove and I couldn't stand that. One day the police brought him home because he had been caught stealing a pair of gloves in a shop. That was a real shock. The gloves were returned straight away to the shop of course. His face red with shame he appeared at our door escorted by the police. 'Please don't tell dad', he said immediately. I only told Rob years later about it, as I didn't know how he would react at the time."

Rob replied: "She still doesn't tell me things straight away. That's okay really, because in her own way she means well. Of course, when I used to find out eventually, I would say: 'Why didn't you tell me right away, I could've helped out in my own way.' For example regarding the case of the gloves, I would probably have been angry and grounded him for a week or so if I had known."

My oldest darts memory also stems from around this time. We went on a family holiday to Majorca by plane. I think I was 6 or 7 at the time. On the island was an old farmer with a sort of fairground stall. At the back of it were cards you had to try to hit with small darts. I tried it a few times and always won. Every day I used to come home with, either a teddy bear, a Cowboy and Indian's toy or something else that was fun. Most stuff I had to give away because all the prizes wouldn't fit in the suitcase to take on our flight back."

The Van Barneveld family was not rich, but thanks to the holiday coupons from Rob's work, the family was able to enjoy a holiday in Majorca in the early seventies. Rob, with Bianca on his lap, Anneke, Raymond and uncle Cor.

Bianca van Barneveld, Raymond's sister, remembers that holiday and her elder brother's first darts experience very well. "There was a stall on the boulevard where you could throw darts to win a prize. Raymond called it 'mini spear throwing'. Every day, when we walked passed with my uncle Cor, my mother's brother; he wanted to throw some darts. Uncle Cor also had a dartboard at home. Whenever we were there Raymond was allowed to play darts for a while. He loved it. He was only 12 or so at the time.

One of the things he won at the darts stall in Majorca was a Spanish doll. He gave it to me as a present straight away. I don't remember if he had to leave most of his prizes there when we went back home but I do remember that my doll did come home with me."

One word that seems to be repeatedly linked to Raymond's time in Transvaal is: Small. As in the small amount of money there was for fun stuff, like going to an ADO game. The small amount of luggage on holiday, which forced him to leave his precious dart prizes in Spain and the small size of the house he lived in on the Wesselstraat. As the size of this house would contribute to changing his life considerably.

"Our house on the Wesselstraat was very small. I passed by it some years later and thought: my God, how could we have actually lived here. Still, I only have happy memories of that time. There was always something to do, especially in the summer when everybody was outside all day long. Our parents used to sit on the kerbside in front of their doors talking, while we played in the streets. It was a typical working-class district of The Hague.

At home, all my decisions were made for me. My parents never allowed me to go swimming for example. They protected me a lot and all in all I thank them for that. It is what every parent wants to do but of course it wasn't right. It didn't not allow me to gain in confidence. You have to be able to grow up a bit by yourself sometimes, to learn from your own mistakes."

At first, Raymond did really well at school, especially with maths.

"I had a certain knack for maths, numbers, and calculations. We used stage levels to monitor your improvement in mathematics at the time. There were twenty stages in total. Stage 1 was, for example, the correct completion of fifty pages of sums. I was already on stage 14 or 15 when the rest of the class was still on Stage 3. That was quite unusual. Mind you at one point I lost my lead considerably. We had to do fractions and divisions and…Agh! I was lost. I didn't understand it anymore.

Since then, I have always wondered what the actual practical purpose of fractions really is. What do you need them for in everyday life? I have never been in a situation where I needed 2 and ? parts of anything. Have you? So why did we have to learn it? I couldn't handle it. So the rest of the class caught up with me at that point.

My life of fun, up until now, ended abruptly when I was 9 years old. Suddenly, my father managed to secure a house on the Gedempte Burgwal in the centre of The Hague. It came as a big surprise, it was a quick decision. I was in year 4 when all of a sudden I heard the news that we were going to move. I remember shedding lots of tears at the time, especially when I had to say goodbye to my friends, I was crying my eyes out. The problem was keeping in touch. Those were different times indeed. Nowadays you have mobile phones, the internet, etc. You can keep in touch wherever you are. Back in those days of course we didn't have such devices. I left the neighbourhood and that was the end of that. It upset me a lot.

In and around this new neighbourhood I only managed to find one new friend and after just three years there, he moved away! It was a very busy street with a lot of bustling city traffic and shoppers constantly moving around from morning to night, so I could not play outside. When there is a group of you together, you learn a lot more about life, like with me and the gang on the Wesselstraat. One says this and another says that and you learn from each other. If you only have one friend in your street and then he leaves, there is nothing left. I can remember that from when I was about 12 up to when I was around 20, I was always on my own. True I had my sister Bianca at home but we had a big house and didn't play together a lot. Once in a while a friend would come over but he went to a different school and didn't live in our neighbourhood, so time together was limited. I also found it difficult to adjust to a new school and mix easily with the other boys and girls. That was quite a big deal and affected me a lot at the time.

One big advantage my dad had over a lot of other people was that he was incredibly clever with his hands. We used to have a craze on these Lone Ranger figures and the whole neighbourhood collected them. You could also buy horses and a matching stable. My dad made me a similar one, out of wood and all of a sudden I was the most popular boy in the street! Nobody else had one, because it cost Dfl 150 in the shops and this was far too expensive for most people. Yes, my dad could make anything like that."

Raymond has mixed memories about his father Rob. On the one hand, he could be a sweet and caring father who had Raymond's best interests in mind but on the other hand, Rob could also be very strict forbidding him a lot of things. These extremes influenced the father and son relationship accordingly.

Rob van Barneveld was adopted and his adoptive parents gave him a strict upbringing. His girlfriend at the time, Anneke became pregnant in the summer of 1966. They married quickly, in January 1967. Not long after the ceremony, Raymond was born.

Rob: "One of our favourite TV series was called Ironside. We used to watch it a lot. The lead character was Raymond Burr and this was the reason that we gave him this name. Raymond was an incredibly sweet and quiet boy. But there always seemed to be something going on with him. For example when he was two he nearly died from a feverish convulsion. One day there was a birthday party being held by someone in Anneke's family, so after work I went there. The room was full of visitors and Raymond was there too. I picked him up and gave him a kiss. He seemed really hot so we put him straight to bed. All of a sudden though his eyes started to roll to the side and he became still and quiet. Someone suggested that we take him to the hospital straight away but I was in such a state I couldn't drive. I didn't even have a car. My brother in law Jan then in a instant piled us all into his car and drove us from the Schilderswijk to the Juliana Kinderziekenhuis, the local children's hospital, a good twenty-minute drive away. Jan gave his car full throttle, ignoring any red lights that seemed to appear, then disappear behind us in a flash. All seemed to be going well until we hit a street junction with the Laan van Meerdervoort. Bang! We hit another car. The other car looked a total loss. Jan's car although smashed-up was still going, so he drove on and guess what, a little further down the road we noticed a police car following us. We found out later that they had been called to the scene of the crash and had followed the trail of Jan's leaking radiator in an effort to apprehend him. Raymond was almost choking in the back of the car in the beginning but strangely enough the force of the collision had helped dislodge some slime that had been stuck in his throat and now he was breathing a lot better again. Jan was already giving Raymond mouth-to-mouth resuscitation but after the collision Ray was able to breathe again. The police then promptly escorted us to the hospital where Raymond received further treatment. That was the worst convulsion he ever had."

A few years later, little Raymond had another brief encounter with death, his father relates: "It was early one Sunday morning during the summer, about six a.m., I think. I had to go to the bathroom and I thought that all the family was still asleep. In the Wesselstraat we had a hallway which ran along for six metres, covered with lino. All of a sudden I heard the patter of tiny feet in the kitchen. As the toilet was next to the kitchen and there was no door leading into the kitchen, I could hear everything going on perfectly. All of a sudden 'click, clunk'. Raymond was taking something out of the fridge. That little trick was not allowed in our house, he couldn't just get food from the fridge without asking but Raymond was hungry. I stood there for a few moments and then heard a rustle. I was laughing to myself. What if he knew I was an audience to this whole episode?

Suddenly though I heard him gasping for breath and making funny choking noises. It turned out that a slice of roast beef had got lodged in his throat. His hunger had nearly got the better of him but extremely luckily for him I was close-by. I ran straight in, put my fingers down his throat and just about managed to extract the meat-slice. Another very close shave for Raymond. He was already turning blue. I really thought he was choking to death at the time. I started crying when it was over because I really thought he was going to die."

Rob Van Barneveld brought his two children up well in a lot of ways, emphasising politeness for one. "They were taught to remember to say 'hello' when they came in or met someone and say 'thank you' when they were given something. Also never to take something to eat from the dinner table before it was offered. I wanted them to listen and you know, they really did! I had great kids. Of course there were difficult moment's occasionally but no real trouble, you understand. I sometimes reminisce about Raymond and when he was small. He had a special affinity with his toys and loved them a lot. Just like I did when I was young. Trains, cars, the works. Back in those days, there was a brand of toys called MatchBox who made die cast toys, including cars. The Haagse Market had toy stalls which sold these types of cars fairly cheap. So every Friday on the way home from work, I used to buy a couple. We started collecting them and it went on for weeks and weeks. Once I came home from work sick and I can remember Ray was used to getting his cars every Friday by now. 'Where are they?' he cried out. 'Look I'm very sick son, I will pick them up tomorrow morning, okay.' He threw a tantrum because he wanted his new car's right there and then. That was it. He didn't get another car ever from me. Because I believe that kind of behaviour is not right.

Of course over the years we collected and saved many other toys and things. He got this trait from me I think and he inherited his sweet and calm nature from his mother. Yes, she is a very good and kind person."

'Sinterklaas', St Nicholas, always celebrated on the 5th of December in The Netherlands, mainly focused on the children of the household. Even though money was tight, the Van Barneveld children always received a lot of presents on that day.

Gedempte Burgwal, The Hague

The move to the large house on the Gedempte Burgwal was to be a huge and difficult step in Raymond's life. No more hanging out in the street. No more friends to play with either. Ironically in a strange way, the extra living space did not agree with him. He couldn't get used to his new environment and withdrew into himself. Likewise having to become a member of a new class in a new school, mixing with a lot of children he didn't know, was a big trial for the shy, introverted Raymond.

"From the minute we left the Wesselstraat, my happy childhood imploded. The only highlights were mine and my sister's outings, visiting family, aunts and uncles. Sometimes we were allowed to spend the night with them. My grandparents on my mother's side had six or seven children. Maybe it is not nice to say but at Christmas it was a lot nicer there than with my grandparents on my fathers side. He was an only child and therefore we were the only family that went there. I was already about 16 before the first nephew on my mother's side came along. I know Grandma and Grandpa Van Barneveld did everything they could to make it fun for us when we visited but they were very old already.

When we used to stop off at my other grandparents, there were normally lots of aunts and uncles there who were still quite young, only twenty or just touching thirty. That was a lot livelier. However, when my parents were going out for the evening or away for a weekend, my sister and I mainly had to stay with Grandma and Grandpa Van Barneveld. As we didn't like to go there much, especially when we were children, I would take my boxes of Playmobil and Lego with me to help pass the time, playing on my own. Santa Claus was fun though. As I said, my parents didn't have much, but we did get a lot of presents! Also at birthdays and on Christmas Day. I remember the best present ever: a guitar with a shoulder strap. I was mad about *The Sweet*. Especially their song called *Wig Wam Bam,* it was my favourite. When I saw them perform it on television I wanted to copy their act. My father would usually ask me in advance what I wanted for my birthday and each time I replied: a guitar with a strap. So one year that's exactly what I got on my birthday, together with a small amplifier. My mother had already given me some new clothes as a present. So when I got the guitar, I had to dress up and perform, Ah! My father played the *Wig Wam* record and I did a playback mime for them. Rock-on Barney you say! I still love music and I enjoy singing along with the car radio. I don't know if my voice is any good but Silvia says it is. Put it this way, nobody has ever got out of the car because of it, so far!

Raymond and Bianca help decorate the Christmas tree.

"It is true we didn't have a lot of friends on the Gedempte Burgwal", says his **sister Bianca**. "The children across the road moved away soon after we arrived. I didn't like the house much either, just like Raymond. It seemed too large, dark and scary. Of course objectively it was a lovely house, especially with all the things my father did to it but I never really liked it there. The only advantage was that we were very close to the city centre with all its shops and department stores. In those days though Sundays were really Sundays! No shops open, nothing to do. Everything was much quieter. That day seemed to last forever. Raymond and I truly hated Sundays but at least he was still able to go and play darts on Sunday as he got older. I had nothing to do all day long."

As is the way with many siblings, things didn't always go smoothly between brother and sister. "Once we were colouring and we each had our own pack of felt-tip pens. When his red pen ran out, he took mine. Then when I wanted it back he said it was his! I don't remember whether it actually was or not, but we had a BIG fight about it. During the squabble he swung out and hit me in the face, giving me a nosebleed. I remember remarking that we had another red to use for colouring now but of course I also cried. I think that was the only time Raymond and I had a real fight."

Bianca clearly remembers the red guitar: "Yes, he played it all day long.

The little red guitar with the black strap that Raymond used to play on.

Singing *Wig Wam Bam*, great. Really good. I couldn't get enough of him singing that song. He's a pretty good singer, just like me. When they recorded a CD a few years ago with all the darts players singing, you could hear that he's got a pretty good voice. We both seem to have a knack, that when we have heard a song just two or three times, we can already sing along with it quite easily.

At meal times, Raymond was a clown. He used to love comedy and was a great impersonator. He also managed to put his own slant on the characters' humour and had us all laughing and falling about round the table each time."

I can still remember my first day at my new school, the K. Ter Laanschool. Perhaps this was the period that is still at the root of my uncertainty. Up until the age of 9, I never felt unsure of my ability to do well and I always knew what I wanted. At the new school though, it turned out, that previously I had learned maths and reading in a different way to how it was taught there. Unfortunately for me the teacher, very early on, with the good intention of involving me I must add, asked me in front of forty children, to whom at the time I was a perfect stranger, to solve a maths question. I gave the wrong answer and was laughed at by 39 children.

So what happened? I became afraid of answering any questions. When, just two days later, the teacher asked me a similar question, I was so afraid of giving a wrong answer that I wouldn't reply and again became the laughing stock of the whole class immediately.

Naturally these experiences influence your whole life. I didn't want to do or try anything anymore, certainly not at school. I built a mental barrier to keep myself safe. I kept it up for years. At school things went downhill pretty quickly from then on. It all stemmed from my lack of confidence. I think now that I am a lot smarter than my CITO Test, a form of 11+ showed up at the time. I was sent to the Lower Technical School, LTS, sort of similar to a craftsman's streamed class in a Secondary Modern. It was a great shame as I felt that up until I was nine I was a capable and good student. After the move, I just lost interest."

"Yes, Raymond was 9 when we moved into our new house on the Gedempte Burgwal", **father Rob** remembers. "I never got the impression that he didn't like it though. On the contrary, on the Wesselstraat he and Bianca shared a two by two metre room and the door opened in as well. However in this new, large three-storey house they both had quite a big room. In fact there was plenty of space for us and the kids. Raymond was given the attic room which was about 20 foot deep. I took down all the partioning walls up there for him to make the room even bigger. He played with his Playmobil there a lot. Every night we played a sort of indoor football. There was enough room for it. After dinner you could easily sweat off your evening meal up there. Although I must say that we punctured a lot of balls in the process on the bare nails.

There was also a time when we used to play chess, twice a day. I was always giving Raymond a lot of attention. On Saturdays we used to go out for lunch together. We would have a bowl of soup with some rolls. Then he would imitate Dutch comedians. He had a style that was like a cross between Norman Wisdom and Benny Hill. He was really good at it and we used to laugh our heads off together. A lot of people don't know the real Raymond. He is full of humour, he can be really funny."

Raymond grew into an insecure teenager that had no idea how to behave around girls.

Humour or not, his time spent at the K. ter Laan school was to mark the onset of a less agreeable period for Raymond. A lack of confidence, friendship and a consuming fear of the unknown, turned the smiling happy go lucky young boy from The Hague into an insecure adolescent.

"I was tested to enter the Lower Technical School (LTS) stream at the Vlietschool in Voorburg along with a few other junior school classmates. There were several other co-ed schools in the area but for one reason or another I was not accepted into any of them. I had to find another school, once again, where I didn't know anyone. I eventually went to the Laakkade. Where there was not a co-ed school in sight. After two years there, I had to choose the best subject to specialise in. What should or could I take? Metalwork, electrics, painting or carpentry? At the time I thought it might be wise to choose carpentry, mainly because my father knew a lot about it. Then, I thought, he could help me if I didn't understand anything. As whatever my father sees, his hands can make. He's a true craftsman. I didn't seem to have inherited this skill. I could never get the hang of it.

I really didn't like it at that school either. Sometimes I had four hours of carpentry, one hour after another, on and on, horrible, really! I can truly say that I did not enjoy one single day at that school. The trouble was that I couldn't really say that at home when I got home. Some people go to technical schools and become, say, a car mechanic. So when you have trouble with your car, at least you know what the problem is and can fix it. That I find useful and maybe I should have chosen that subject instead, as my skill in carpentry did not seem to be of any use at all. Although what do you really know when you are young? My father was a carpenter and because I didn't feel comfortable in choosing for myself, I became one too.

We led a simple life really, we only had Nederland 1 and 2 on the Box and that was that. I was pretty naive and lived in my own little world where I would play darts or just sit in my room in the attic mucking about. Fortunately it was a large attic where I could play football on my own to my heart's content. I never thought any further than the next day.

The LTS I went to was a boy's only school. Eighty percent of the secondary schools in those days were mixed, boys and girls together but mine wasn't. So when eventually I would summon up all my courage and join some friends going to a disco, I was not used to approaching the girls. I didn't know what to say or do or how to act at all. Maybe a girl or two might have smiled at me or something, but I never cottoned-on at the time. I had no idea what to do and that frustrated me enormously. I was not infatuated or in love with any girls, even from a distance but I did want to be one of the boys, naturally. I didn't even have the hots for a movie star. A bit sad really, looking back. I was very behind the curve. I didn't know what to do with my life, I had no idea of what I wanted to be when I grew up, so I just did anything as it came along. I was so naive that, for example, I went to a shop to buy a bicycle once. I liked the blue one but my friend who was with me recommended the green one, so I went home with the green bike, didn't I! I was far too easily influenced then and for years I didn't manage to form any opinions of my own at all. On the contrary I found what other people thought much more important.

This characteristic was formed in those days and has stayed with me. I am still quite easily influenced. Fortunately however not as much as before because I have gained a bit more confidence in these recent years.

Van Barneveld, the Keeper (looking at the photo, fourth from the right standing) with the famous championship winning football team H.V.V. De Adelaars. Raymond was a pretty good football player. His teacher said he would go far.

I didn't have any friends in those days but never stopped to think about it much. I played football with De Adelaars and Oranje-Blauw but I never even got to know anybody at football enough to pal up with and play around. The idea simply didn't occur to me. I can't remember having dinner at a footballing friend's house, ever. I think I was good at playing football. Right up until we moved house I played really well. At school, I seemed to have the Midas touch, as each time I kicked the ball it would fly into the net. One of my teachers said I could become a very good player. Well ... that didn't happen of course and my insecurity undoubtedly played a part in that. I used to keep goal but also played as a striker or right mid-field even. Not really a position for a somewhat slow player like me. In the end I didn't develop into a good football player, probably due to my mix of passiveness and naivety. A lot of the time I would just stand there waiting for the ball to come along, and when it did I would nonchalantly look around for someone to pass to. By then one of the other team would have quickly robbed me of the ball. Easy. I was just not able to raise the fighting spirit in me. When there was a party at the football club, they used to say to me: 'Just turn up, there will be lots of nice girls there.' Well, I didn't. I was too apprehensive. I still am very shy, although I may not come across that way. I never took the initiative to reach out to people, not even to friends at school. For me it was 'Just friends at school and no further.' The rest of my life was private. I never had any boys from school stay-over at my place. When I look at my son Mike and the way he knocks about with his friends, I think to myself, he's nothing like me. Sometimes I feel a bit jealous when I hear the stories from my children and Silvia. I listen to how Silvia grew up in an area with lots of boys and girls. They had parties, dancing and dating, the lot! I never experienced that. Sometimes I think to myself: 'S**t, I have missed a lot in my life, haven't I? If everything had worked out differently, I might be a smooth talker now.' It was so easy to pull the wool over my eyes in those days. On the other hand, maybe it did me a lot of good. It did make me spend a lot of time in my attic, training. My darting ability started to rise considerably during that time. But the price was being paid for in another area of my life.' It seems true what they say, that here are no short cuts in life."

"Raymond was never a star player at football", remarks his **sister Bianca**. "He always joined in when they played it on the holiday campsite though. Once, he scored all the goals for his side during a tournament, including the winning goal in the final. That day he played like a man possessed! Everyone was taken-a-back.

There was always something happening on the campsite. Raymond was not always around though because at that time he already played darts a lot. When he was around though, life was never boring! One night we *escaped* from our tents and went into the local village. Of course my parents didn't know anything about it. We were all about 16 at the time and there were ten of us in total. It was quite a long walk into the village and on the way we took a few flags from the flagpoles that we passed. Raymond didn't join in but everybody else did. In reality we had stolen the flags, well, stolen? As we walked on a police car passed by. They were not looking for any one particularly but they just happened to be passing. But we all ran off frightened, because that's how it goes doesn't it. By the roadside was a wall of about 3 foot wide and 3 foot high. Raymond was fairly tall already, consequently, when he tried to hide behind the wall, bits of him were sticking out on all sides.

A football playing Van Barneveld in his Oranje-Blauw outfit. "Playing at right-back was not the ideal position for Raymond: The ball had to come to him instead of the other way around," declared Rob Van Barneveld.

We ran on and as I looked back at what was going on I started to giggle straight away. When we called him to get up and keep running, he stood up and joined us. When I glanced back again, I saw him lagging way behind. I shouted at him to hurry up but when he began putting on a spurt he fell to the ground and strained his ankle. We were all laughing like crazy but he was getting very angry. We carried on running and then, for goodness sake, when I looked to see if he was keeping up now, I saw that he had pulled up because he had twisted his ankle again. He went ballistic because I crumpled in a heap laughing at him."

A young Raymond in his tent at the campsite. He could hardly fit in, with his long legs.

"Playing football and games", that's how **Rob** describes the childhood of his son. "Raymond was a reasonably good football player but he was a bit passive. When he was growing up playing the sport, he would wait far too long for the ball to come to him. When it did happen, he knew how to handle the play-off quite well. I'd have preferred him to go to the ball more. Raymond was a pretty good player overall though, because he was so tall. He could easily shrug off any opponents. I used to go and watch him every Saturday but didn't want to be a coach for his team, because it would have been difficult not to start favouring him over others. I like things to be fair and square. Raymond has this in him too. He can't stand cheats but I must say he also can't stand losing.

For example we often played Stratego, a tactical battlefield board game. One day I had him nailed. In the game you normally place the spy directly behind the general in order to defend yourself. The spy by the way is the only one who can beat the marshal, who in turn is the highest-ranking soldier in the game. Just for the fun of it though,

I put an explorer behind my general and then the spy. At that point he moved in with his marshal to slay, what he thought was my spy. Of course it was a wrong move, as with the next move I slayed his marshal. He was so furious that he threw the board away, there and then."

Being a bad loser is not such a bad characteristic for a sportsman to have though, when channelled positively. The mastering of this potentially negatively charged emotion into a positive one, became the drive behind his will to win. Even at a young age, winning became all-important to him. It helped him to balance out his frustrations and build up his sense of self-worth. The catalyst came through darts, which started to play an increasingly important role in his life as he got older.

"When I wasn't playing darts by myself, I was busy with my other hobbies of collecting stamps and coins. I could really lose myself in these pastimes. I can't recall exactly how I started collecting. By living on the Gedempte Burgwal everything was close at hand. I often walked through the city centre where all the shops were, including the big ones; V&D's, C&A's. I also collected stickers and used to ask everyone for them. I remember that one of the local kids had a stamp collection and some spare stamps. I bought a bag full of them from him. First I had to soak them to get the backing paper off and then I bought an album to put them all in. It was only then that I found out, I had actually purchased a bag full of worthless gap fillers. This angered me but also prompted me to start buying better quality and more expensive stamps. I spent all my money on stamp collecting at one stage. Pocket money, birthday money, everything went on this craze. Actually, I still have my collections of stamps and coins but don't look at them or do anything with them anymore. If I wanted to sell them now, they would probably go for next to nothing. The problem with collecting was that it was never enough. The watershed arose when two stamps were released at he same time, stuck on the same envelope, called a *Doorloper* in Dutch. Of course they were worth more. But they also cost more! Then they released another envelope with TWO Doorlopers stamped and posted on a special day. Now in those days it was impossible for a boy my age to see the bigger picture. I wanted to have the best collection possible but also knew that I could no longer afford it. It really was becoming an obsession. So at about 16 I said to myself 'Enough!' I put everything in a cupboard and have never looked at it again! But I still have all the stuff I collected, except for my original Panini books with all my football cards. My father threw them all out one day. You see, once or twice a year my father held what we called a national clean-up Sunday. There and then, on the day, he would throw everything out he considered worthless. I tell you, year in year out I collected these books and stuck the cards in and one day he just threw them all out! They must be worth a fortune nowadays and to make matters worse, he always teased me about it afterwards. He used to say: 'Raymond, remember your football cards? You made me throw them out didn't you?' The hair would stand up on the back of my neck. That really got to me. As, mixed in with those cards and books, were a lot of memories of my youth. And he just threw them out…

Fifteen or twenty books, gone in one throw! He just threw away a big, important and pleasant chunk of my not so nice childhood, there right in front of me. When I brought it up from time to time later, he never seemed to quite understand what I was talking about. Now he does though, as when I turned forty, he gave me two series of Panini books for my birthday. He said at the time that from then on he didn't want to hear anymore about it, ever again but I couldn't promise him that.

A quote from Raymond's father, **Rob** about the Panini book saga: "Yes, for years he kept on nagging me about it. 'Remember, oldie,' he used to say, 'remember the night you threw them out? Just like that.' So eventually, in the spring of 2007, I went on the internet and saw the series of books for sale, The Complete '74 World Cup and The glory years of Ajax. I bought them. Then when I gave them to him as a present, I also said jokingly: 'Just one thing before you unwrap them, now I don't want to hear anymore about this event, okay.' 'I know that already!' he replied in turn."

Trading football cards at school with the boys was a passionate, fun hobby. Especially because I loved football. This passion has never left me. Not playing myself I mean but as a spectator. Not that I would stand there on the touchline though, week in week out. I have never made the effort to go somewhere and watch a team regularly, although I do love the game itself. On occasions I used to go and see ADO Den Haag play but not regularly, not even now, as I am rarely home these days. At the times that I managed to go to ADO, I would go with my darts buddy Dick Pronk. We used to stand together on the *Midden Noord,* the Middle North Terrace, a very notable name in Dutch football circles.

Anyway, after I met Silvia, I had her to discuss and confide in about all these past events in my life. About the time living on the Gedempte Burgwal when a lot went wrong with me. The way I started to doubt myself. Dreading the days I had to write an essay, or stand up and say something in school. For days beforehand I couldn't sleep. Speaking in public? I was terrified. My dad helped me with these presentations. My mother also wanted to help but she had left school at the end of year 5 in the Dutch 'Lagere school', as she had to go to work. The poor woman never got the chance of a good education at all. Fortunately nowadays this doesn't happen anymore. On the contrary children seem so wise these days. If I took my daughters out of school now to go to work, they would probably be fine. But in the old days it was very different. When my mother was young she had to work hard from eight in the morning until nine in the evening each day, day after day after day. There was no time or money for the luxury of a good school education. My father however, grew up in a different, more privileged world. My mother did, in the end, also manage to develop and cope with life, just fine. If you were to meet her now, you would realise that she has become a very refined lady and I admire her for that. In the same way I admire the fact that she was always there for us. She gave so much love and affection, mainly because I spent so much time at home.

She always cooked food we enjoyed but we were not close the way I was with my father, going out together to my local football club and things like that. My mother didn't have a driving licence for a start so that made it a lot more difficult to go anywhere together. When we went out we always had to take a local tram or bus, then change buses, etc. She did still manage to spoil me a lot though. For example I was 18 or 20 before I made my own sandwiches. They were always there ready for me.

When we went to the K. ter Laanschool in the Bezemstraat, there was a HEMA, a Dutch department store with a small snack bar in front of it, just around the corner from where we lived. My mother used to buy us snacks from there to eat at lunchtime. As money was short sometimes when my father was struggling to get work, he didn't approve of this, as it was rather expensive. For a few days we would eat plain sandwiches. As my sister and I didn't like them much and said so all the time, we were soon back to eating our snacks.

Apparently mum would arrange the up-grade, behind my father's back. Purely out of love for us, she is such a sweet person.

I think I have inherited the more calmer, passive nature of my mother. She's the type to go to the butcher, take a queue-ticket but then let five people go in front of her, if they were in a hurry. She does not mind waiting and she would also just want to keep the peace. I was and still am a bit like that as well. I never liked confrontations or squabbles; I always wanted other people to like me. But now I know a lot more about life. I know that this kind of outlook won't get you very far, especially in darts. I slowly learned how to stand up for myself. Some people didn't appreciate that, too bad. My mother can't do that. On the one hand, you could argue that passivity is a good thing but on the other I think she has missed out a lot by acting the way she does. The same way I did for all those years. I still find that frustrating.

Most days I used to stay in my large attic bedroom, playing darts. Sometimes I made up tournaments or sports events. For example, I used to take a piece of paper and write down 32 names of football teams. I'd screw them up into little balls and put them all together, then play out an imaginary European Cup lottery. On each piece of paper I wrote, European Cup I, first round; Barcelona v Bayern München and so on. Later on in the game things got more difficult because I realised that I also needed results! So, how would I get them? I quickly thought of a solution. I took a die and rolled it each time to produce the number of goals scored per team. Six was changed to equal zero, otherwise you got weird results and would also imply that the goalie was no good! Know what I mean Edwin. I rolled the die first for Barcelona, who for example would show as a 1 and then roll a 2 for Bayern Munich. That was classed as the result of the match but, ah, yes, they had to play home and away... So I ended up doing all these fixtures until there were only sixteen teams left. Then I made another 16 balls of paper and so on, frittering whole afternoons away, just doing that.

I used the same idea with darts basically. I would write 32 names down, including Bristow, Lowe, Anderson and Van Barneveld of course and then I would throw for all of them myself. Each player was allowed three throws at the 20. For example I might have thrown 100, 60 and 85. Then came John Lowe's turn, who scored 245 points. He was playing against Cliff Lazarenko and he threw 100, 100 and a 41. So Cliff lost by 4 points. That's how I played it. Of course, I made an extra effort when playing myself! That's logical. In fact that might have formed the basis of how I play now, come to think of it. Maybe it sounds a lonely existence to some, but I enjoyed it. My imagination made a quantum leap during those years. Also I didn't have a girlfriend, so I had all the time in the world to do these kinds of things.

Something good happened during that time too. My parents bought a caravan that was situated on the Familieland campsite in Hoogerheide. It was there, eventually, that I did find some friends. I was 16 or 17 when they bought the caravan and by that time I had already started to compete in various darts tournaments. Unfortunately I had to stay at home quite frequently in order to play, which was a bit of a shame, having found some mates at last.

I also enjoyed watching television. When we lived on the Wesselstraat my favourites were *Kunt u ons de weg naar Hamelen vertellen, meneer?* And *Wicky de Viking*. On the Gedempte Burgwal we were able to be connected to cable TV for the first time. Wow, all of a sudden we could watch Belgian and German TV as well as the Dutch channels. …And an English station too: BBC 1. That's when I first saw darts on the TV. In 1985 I went over to the UK to watch my first Embassy. I was already playing quite well at the time and everybody was talking about this tournament. So I went over and watched it live, in person. Fabulous! That year, Eric Bristow won the final beating John Lowe 6-2."

Other goings-on took place in our attic room too, remembers **Anneke, Ray's mother**. "While he was living at the house on the Gedempte Burgwal Raymond was sparring with Rob, practicing the taekwondo kicks he was learning at the local sports school. This went on for a while. Suddenly Raymond pivoted, swivelled round and at the same moment kicked his leg up and outwards, accidentally giving his dad a big thump. He didn't mean to hit him I think but his judgement was wrong. Rob just went down, flat out.

'You've now got your own back', I yelled out. A few years before, Rob had floored Raymond with a swinging punch bag. Raymond wanted to learn to box at the time. The incident occurred when Raymond was waiting to start. Rob walked to the side of the room and sneakily pulled back the bag in the opposite direction to where Raymond was standing. 'Are you ready?' he asked Raymond. When he said yes, Rob let go of the punch bag, hitting Raymond full in the face and so down he went, flat. Rob was killing himself laughing but Raymond had had enough and decided that he did not want to box anymore after that."

Over the weekends Raymond often played darts. This meant that he couldn't always go to the caravan in Hoogerheide, the only place where he had found friends, with his parents and sister.

The Van Barneveld family on holiday in Venice during the late seventies.

Father and son

Raymond, who was not always happy with what his father did, is however a lot like him in many ways, but not all. Sometimes Raymond used to be scared of his father but Raymond's children don't think that way of him at all. Also with regard to money Raymond has a different way of handling his children than his father did with him. At least, that is what Raymond thinks, but Rob Van Barneveld has a different opinion about that

"On reflection I find myself pretty boring with regard to fatherhood. I mainly hear myself repeating the things my father said to me all the time. Nothing too bad, more like: lights out, or take your stuff off of the stairs and put it in your room. I only get this rote from my father, not my mother. She always left that kind of stuff to him. As a carpenter he found these things really important to hammer home! All with the best of intentions of course. Sometimes I get strange looks at home when I point these things out. I say mindfully, someone might break their neck coming down the stairs if all this stuff is left on them. That already almost happened once. So prevention is better than cure. That's what my father told me and because I was at home a lot, that's what was drummed into me.

Silvia often says I'm just like my old man. And I am a bit. It's what I am used to. Yes, I used to play in my room or sit in the living room. I have discussed these traits with Silvia a lot. I was often jealous of the children who didn't have a boring childhood. From the age of 9 until I was 20, I was very unhappy and unfortunately I blamed, even as it was unfolding, my parents for that. Especially when my father started out on his new career as a lorry driver. He was gone long and often. My mother didn't have a driving licence so we never went anywhere! We didn't have any spare money for public transport. Sometimes we hitched a ride on the bus or tram without buying a ticket as I wanted to go places. Most of the time however I spent on my own but with hindsight I didn't have a lot of fun, all in all. I missed out on a lot I think.

My father was very strict but at the same time he could be a great guy. He lived for his family and still does. He also provided the money, limited though it was, because a carpenter did not normally make a lot in those days. The downside of this situation was that we could never go on holiday, simply because we did not have the money. So I could never do what a lot of the other children did. Once I met a boy whose father had a snack bar. Strik his name was. He lived around the corner on the Paviljoensgracht. His family were well off so he got to go to the movies every Sunday.

Sometimes I was able to go along with him but mostly when he came to the door to see if I wanted to go, I couldn't. We just didn't have enough money for such luxuries week in week out. In addition, don't forget there were two of us.

Bianca was friends with his sister and we definitely didn't have money for two tickets in one week. So often we were told 'no'. At school, all my friends usually had a few coins in their pockets but with the twenty cents or so I could normally muster, I could just manage to buy a waffle and a cup of tea. I was allowed 5 guilders pocket money each week but from that I also had to pay for my hobbies. After that, there was not a lot left for eating snacks at school. I don't blame my parents but I was always envious of the others.

One day, as an illustration, I went with a couple of boys to the local snack bar nearby for lunch. The three of them bought French fries and I had to sit there with nothing to eat. I am sure my parents would get very emotional and upset were I to confront them with that now, but that is how it was. Those experiences have made me into who I am now. I blame myself too, because I never tried to get a job at the time. I could maybe, with hindsight have delivered papers or try to work somewhere to earn a bit of money. Unfortunately, I didn't have it in me to think about those kinds of things. I also didn't have friends that had jobs themselves to point that out to me. So I made do with my 5 guilders pocket money per week, topped up with any birthday money that came along. Apart from these two sources I had nothing else coming in. Well, yes, because my father was a carpenter, once in a while I could also do a little job for him and then I would get a bit extra which I would put away. Look, to keep things a bit in perspective, 5 guilders seemed a fair bit of money for a young boy to have each week at that time but in reality in those days a ticket for the cinema would already cost, exactly 5 guilders. What do you do for the rest of the week then? Looking at my own children now, I can see that money doesn't go very far. I had to choose between going to a movie once a week, or eating French fries at school twice a week and then still try to eek out enough to buy stamps regularly for my collection.

Rob, Raymond's father says: "Raymond still thinks we couldn't afford much in those days and that surprises and shocks me a bit. No money, no holidays? We went everywhere. I have always spent every penny that I earned on my family. At times I made good money, you know. At Christmas time they used to have a lot of presents. Everything you might imagine would lay under the tree, as well as an envelope each with 250 guilders in it. It started with those Matchbox cars. You need money to keep that going. Each first-day cover, coins, you name it, he got it and also Bianca did too of course. But his actual pocket money of 5 guilders, yes, he had to make do with that."

In those days I decided that I would make sure my children did not have to cope with those kind of problems. And I believe that I succeeded. Thanks also to people who were behind me and supported me through tough times. Now I keep telling my children that not everybody has it so good. I am still not really sure if it goes in. When their pocket money is gone, we always give them some extra. That's because I didn't have that as a child, it's a reaction. Because of the things I missed when young, I now have an urge to have the latest electronic gadgets when they come out. Immediately after it was released I bought Playstation 3. My daughter Daisy said at the time: 'No, not now dad, wait until they are cheaper', but I just wanted it, so I bought it."

Because of his urge to collect things Raymond went against his father's wishes once and he paid for it dearly. Rob used to get angry when he was drunk which used to cause a lot of problems. But by the same token Rob also let his son accompany him to his construction work, instead of going to school sometimes.

"My dad wasn't easy. I remember that all of a sudden I wasn't allowed to collect football cards anymore, just because he felt it was a waste of money. That happened long before he threw all my albums out. Then, just in case he thought I would go behind his back and keep on collecting them, he said literally: 'If I ever find out that you are still buying them, I will tear up the books right in front of you.' Later of course, when he did find out that I had gone behind his back and was still collecting them, he made me go and get the book from the attic. He then did tear it apart, into shreds, right in front of my face just as he said he would! That broke my heart at the time. But if I am honest now, he was right. I had been warned. I broke the rules and got punished accordingly. Funny but I act the same now with my son Mike as my father did with me. That's the only way I have been taught and know. Mike has started playing darts as well now and I just tell him frankly that he is no good at it yet. That's a fact, black and white. I could boost his ego and tell him that he is great when he is not but nothing he has shown me so far makes me think 'wow'. So maybe he will turn out to be as good at darts as I was at carpentry. Who knows, I don't know and I don't mind either way. At the end of the day he has to do what he wants to do. I don't want to be the one who shows him the ropes in the darts world though. I had to learn it all myself, so I think he should too. When he wins, that's great and if he needs a bit of money to play in tournaments he will get it.

Sometimes I used to go out with my father and we would have a great time. When I reminded him that I had to go to school again the following day, he would allow me to stay at home, for a week occasionally. He would just write me a note. That was great. We would do fun stuff together all week long. I might go with him on a carpentry job and follow him around at his work all week. It was wrong of course to bunk-off but he said in its defence that I might as well learn the trade from him as opposed to school.

"Raymond enjoyed being at work with me", **Rob** remembers. "But he also earned a bit of money by tagging along. I will never forget the big job I had in the city. Three, four rooms and a kitchen but four storeys high, with no elevator and wide stairs. All the plasterboard had to be carried up the stairs. So I asked Raymond and one of his friends to come along and help. Their job was to hump all the plasterboard upstairs. I paid them Dfl 100 for doing it. They started at seven thirty and finished four hours later. 'Dad, can I have my money please', Raymond shouted. They did the work in no time; I was caught-out big time there!"

My dad has another side. He's a man with two different attitudes. On the one hand he was a wonderful father to his family and children. He did lay down the law at times but also did everything within his power to look after us and give us the things we wanted. But when he had had a drink, he became tormented, like he had fuelled up a dormant fiend inside him into action. Every Friday or Saturday he used to go out. I must say that he didn't always come home in a rage but when he did, he really scared me. Of course it did, especially when I was little. A person can change a lot when they have had too much to drink. What happened when he came home on a bad night? A lot of shouting and he became alarmingly dictatorial.

I remember I was out of work once and had stayed at home for a couple of days, doing nothing. He couldn't stand that, even in a sober state. So that evening, when he got home after a night out on the town, he came upstairs and made me get out of bed in the middle of the night, saying: 'Go find a job!' 'Do this, do that'. He was shouting and shouting and I was only just half-awake. Sometimes he would come home deep into the night with a little snack for my mother. But when she said she didn't want it, which makes a lot of sense at 2 o'clock in the morning, he was furious. He would shout out at the top of his voice. In his state of mind he thought he deserved praise by bringing her back a snack but who would want to be woken up in order to eat, in the middle of the night? He went completely nuts.

Now my father is in his sixties, I think he must realise what he did to us then, upset us a lot.

I have tried to get to the bottom of it all. Grandpa and Grandma Van Barneveld were both already in their 40's when they adopted my father. His biological mother had had an affair with an American soldier during the Second World War and as a result my father was born. She gave him away for adoption and grandpa and grandma Van Barneveld took him in. My father did not have any cousins or aunts and uncles so he spent his whole youth without much of a family. When he wanted to play with his cars, he had to put an old cloth on the table. My grandmother had put a plastic sheet on it already but the car tyres made marks on that. Well, try to play with your cars on a tablecloth. Yes, they were very strict with him. There was only one day in his whole life that he didn't have to go to school. It was when he had a high fever and couldn't stop vomiting. Even then, my grandmother still wanted to take him! When these are the examples that you grow up with, you use them with your own children too. Yet my father was not always so strict. He did teach me how to play chess and Stratego. I must say that I was a poor loser though, even in those days. I would quite easily tip the board over if I lost my spy at Stratego or my queen at chess. Of course I got a smack round the head when that sort of thing happened, and was sent straight up to bed as punishment. I do feel though the fact that I have some American pioneering blood running through my veins could be a logical explanation for my strong will to win. I am very fond of that country as it stands.

Raymond and Bianca visiting Oma Van Barneveld. Opa and Oma Van Barneveld adopted Rob when they were already in their forties.

My father was hardened by life. For example outside our house on the Gedempte Burgwal mandatory paid parking was introduced while we lived there. He had to wait a long time for a parking permit and could not find a parking spot anywhere nearby. So he started parking illegally, right in front of the door. Every day he parked there a fine of 35 guilders was slapped on his windscreen. So in no time at all we had a huge pile of fines lying on the sideboard. He then decided to take the matter to court. Eventually he won and did not have to pay the fines. But during this time he would drink more. His mind could not stand the stress, the injustice and this was his way of releasing the tension.

These events taken in by the eyes of a seven year old boy had a big impact on me. I was really scared of my dad. I felt really bad when he came home drunk. I often wondered why we never had any spare money for even the simple things in life, when he could afford to go out and do all that drinking."

Rob: "I realise now that I was really annoying and unkind to people when I had had a few drinks. I am sorry about that but unfortunately I can't turn back the clock. I am still, even today, confronted with the memories of those episodes, also by Anneke. It's not that I don't want to hear what I did wrong. Somebody who has had too much to drink tends to change, sometimes for the worse. A large number of people who get drunk can be annoying and irritating, me included. I now wish it could have been different. Once I didn't have a drink for two years but I felt left out socially. I liked a good drink, but didn't have a red light. Everything I did, I did too much of. Raymond definitely hated it when I arrived home the worst for wear, after a few drinks. I understand that I took the wrong path but again, unfortunately, I can't turn back time. Things can be forgiven but maybe not forgotten."

Raymond at the age of 16 playing competitive darts for the first time at The Entertainer – his father's local.

Darts or work?

By practicing a lot, Raymond started to develop his darting talent. He enjoyed it more and more and as a result of winning a local darts competition at the Entertainer café-pub, was able to qualify for his first tournament. He seemed to develop as an exceptional talent quite quickly but, because there was no real money to be made in darts at that time, Raymond had to prepare himself to get a job. He had to earn a living.

"I was able to get my first job through the help of a friend, Michel Klooster, who has now unfortunately passed on. I knew Michel from my time at the K. ter Laanschool. He worked at the Westeinde Hospital in the centre of The Hague. So he helped me apply for a job there as well. Cleaning, Monday to Friday, 2 hours a day from 17:30 to 19:30. Vacuuming, emptying bins, wiping desks. It didn't pay a lot but I needed fuel in the tank for my sports lightweight. I had a Yamaha RD. It was okay, but not the bike I really wanted. That was a Honda MT5. It looked more like a scrambler, which was *the* bike of the moment.And there you go again: I was 16, everyone had one and I didn't. My father said that if I had one it would be stolen from right under my nose. Another frustration had to be absorbed. Especially because I wanted to buy it with the money that my grandmother had saved from my birth to give to me. The whole world had a Honda MT5, and I didn't.

Rob also didn't possess the motorcycle of his dreams when he was younger: "I was the youngest amongst all of my friends. Everyone had a scooter, but I didn't. I wanted a Puch, just like all the others. My father said at the time: 'If you get a Puch you will never have enough money to run it.' I had to live with that statement. On my 16th birthday I got given a scooter. My mother always promised that and my father indeed did buy me one. He did it up himself, in light blue and grey.

What do you know; he came home that day riding the scooter. My birthday. It was mine, yes! However it turned out to be a Union with a Sachs-engine. Not a Puch. How was I supposed to feel going around with the boys? He had set the stupid machine to run at a maximum of 43 kilometres per hour. My friends all drove at 70 kph, even through the sand dunes. They seemed to have to wait for me at the top of every hill.

Later Honda bikes were in and Ray desperately wanted one. He is definitely not technical, so that was not why he wanted it. He must have just found them better looking than the others and everyone had one. The problem was that these Honda's were being stolen left, right and centre. Therefore, I decided he couldn't have one, but definitely not because I thought it would spoil him. I didn't do it to spite him, I just tried to be strict in a fair way. That's not the same as being a father who forces his own views onto others, is it?"

I worked in the hospital for about two years, I even lied a little about my age. You were only allowed to start work at 17 in those days but I was only 16. At one point I was fed up with cleaning, as the floors were constantly in a terribly dirty state. I asked my supervisor if there was any other job I could do apart from this one. Fortunately I managed to get moved. They put me on cleaning the doctor's areas with another worker, a woman, a much easier job. Once, as I was removing a rubbish bag from a bin I caught my hand on a sharp edge.
A tiny dot of blood appeared on my finger but I didn't give it a second thought. In passing, a while later, I mentioned this to a supervisor and he immediately started panicking. He took me straight to First Aid and before I knew it my pants were around my ankles and I had a needle stuck in my backside! I thought: 'Great what's next?' But yes, they didn't want to take any risks. The anti-tetanus injection was of course a good precaution to take but all the fuss surprised me, as the cut was probably caused by the sharp edge of a box or something like that.

I earned Dfl 195 a month. Not really a fantastic amount but for someone who was still of school age, not bad at all.

I got to know a boy named Bert Linnenbank at the LTS. I used to go home with him at lunchtime, eat a sandwich together and chat. He had a dartboard at home to practise on, because he always played at Café Du Burck, on the Hildebrandstraat in The Hague. I never went there with him, but used to play a set with him at his place. I enjoyed it so much I asked my father for a dartboard for my 17th birthday. I got one but it was not the right one. It was one with green and red sections. So my first dartboard had the wrong colours. It should have been black and white. I will never, in my whole life forget this. Anyway with my birthday money I bought a set of Winmau arrows from Perry Sport for Dfl 50. That is how it all started. After this everything went at full speed, into top gear, very quickly.

Around this time I also used to play darts at my uncle Cor Matthee's home quite often. Then one day we started to play Tactics. The game was to aim and hit all the numbers between 10 and 20 and the bull's-eye. Once you have hit a number three times you have *sealed* that number. You can then score points on that number if the other participant has not sealed it themselves yet. To my uncle and father's surprise I started hitting every number I aimed for. This is when I realised for the first time that I had an emerging talent.

My father often went to *The Entertainer*, a bar that was run for years by a couple called Sotir and Jacqueline. He also used to work there sometimes as a carpenter and regularly on a Friday night he used it as his local. I was allowed to go with him sometimes and play a dart set or two with some of the regulars. My father was often told that I was playing some good darts. One day there happened to be a space for a new team. Jacqueline asked my father if he wanted to form and also run the team. He was not very interested at first but Jacqueline insisted that he should do it for me. So a team was formed, consisting of my father, my uncle Hans Kers, a friend of my uncle called Koos Jansen, Humphrey Mutter who was a regular, and me. That was the very first team I was a part of. We called it *The Entertainer Quartet*. We played every Tuesday night. As this was when I still worked at the hospital, my father always used to come and fetch me from there and we would rush down to *The Entertainer* to play.

Moving on a bit, I heard that they also had a doubles tournament every Saturday night. So I used to go there sometimes and play with my uncle Hans. One night we finished as runners-up and I won my first trophy. I was choked up with pride. Also, if you managed to play six Saturday's in a row you were automatically entered into the Café's darts ranking ladder competition. Then you could come into contention to win a prize. The prizes were mostly trophies but later you could sometimes win money too. On Sundays I started playing in The Hague's regional darts ranking competition. There was an A and B pool and also a ladies division. If you played in a local premier division or first division, you took part in the A-pool. If you played in a lower division, you took part in the B-pool. It's from this point, respectively that The Hague's A-team and B-team originated. They played nationally, the same as now with the LaCo, short for Landelijke Competitie, the national competition. It was a great honour in those days to represent your hometown at darts. It's not so much anymore, but at the time The Hague-A was to be feared on The Netherlands darts circuit. We had players such as Pieter Kessels, Rick Daniëls and Gerard Collée. All were tip, top dart players. Playing in The Hague B were most of the future top players of The Netherlands. That was a great time. The boys who started as B-team players and made good, would step over to The Hague-A, normally after about a year.

I will never forget that during my early months and years as a dart player my father was an important influence. He coached me and gave me some tips, which made me five times better than I was. Although having said that, I was still in one respect the same then as I am now, lazy. I always kept thinking that I could still improve without having to put too much effort in. I thought: it will come, it will come. But it didn't come; I really had to invest in myself, in my game. At the time Bert Vlaardingerbroek was THE dart player in The Netherlands. When I played against Bert, my father came with me. I lost 3 sets to 0 and when it was over he walked over to Bert, shook his hand and said: 'Well done, Raymond didn't stand a chance against you. Very well played.' That hit me hard but it was a painful lesson I sorely needed. The same day I went home and trained for 5 hours non-stop in my room. And the day after that again and then again and again. I kept going at it constantly, until eventually I started to beat van Vlaardingerbroek."

Rob: "Raymond thought I had congratulated Bert in order to show him up. That wasn't true. Firstly I was being honest. Bert played to win, and did win. You have to congratulate him on that. Ray did it as well but he was showing himself up as a bad loser. My goal in congratulating Bert at Ray's expense was to motivate him, so that it would encourage him to strive to improve further. Thereby enabling him to perhaps triumph over Bert eventually and I think it worked! Raymond caught the bait and transmuted his uncertainty into strength."

Suddenly Raymond's dart career began to take off. Jan Brouwers, who was seven years older and much more experienced, saw very quickly that Raymond had what it takes and took him under his wing. This period turned out to be crucial for Van Barneveld.

"In 1984 I qualified for a big tournament for the first time. It was The Hague Open. Strangely I was not that nervous. I had never represented the national youth. So from day one I played at senior level and consequently was put to the test immediately, full stop. In this first tournament I made the last 16 which was reasonably good, I thought. Losing to the eventual winner, Paul Hogenboom, narrowly by 3 sets to 2. Prior to the event I had never even heard of him. He said to me afterwards, that our game was the most difficult one for him to win in the whole tournament. It was true, he went on to win the tournament easily after beating me. Next I played in the Groningen Open and then the Breda Open. The fourth tournament that followed was the Rotterdam Open and I won it! My first heavy-weight, high profile Dutch title."

A young Raymond pictured innocently holding his darts in front of a dartboard at his local. Completely oblivious as to how his future darts achievements would change his life.

Raymond and Dick, his wingman from the outset of his darting career, looking very happy standing in Raymond's dart room at home on the Gedempte Burgwal. Behind Dick, in the background is the first award that Raymond ever won, a neat trophy with a blue stem and ribbons. He won it in his local café-bar The Entertainer.

This tournament win in Rotterdam had a remarkable build up to it. Talented Van Barneveld was on the verge of being selected to play for one of the best teams in the country but at the last moment circumstances changed and it didn't happen. This affected him badly and made him extremely fed up. Inside he was furious, burning with anger. Raymond being Raymond though, rose like a phoenix from the ashes and the next day struck in Rotterdam, wiping out the opposition in a savage display of master hood. A decisive moment, heralding his up-coming success, he positively transformed his setback and anger into supreme motivation.

"At the time there was a team in The Hague called the Winmau Diplomats. They were so good that the competition around The Hague was scared of playing them. In fact the whole of The Netherlands was scared stiff of having to play them! They won everything in sight, and virtually always ended up with a 9-0 or 8-1 whitewash victory. The team of 4 consisted of Rick Daniëls, Pieter Kessels, Ellis Elsevijf and Maurice Hoenstok. Every year they were at the top of the Dutch Rankings. The boys were still young. Their trainer, Herman Jongman, always maintained that their victories stemmed from their youth. He was quite a darts visionary, always looking ahead, to the future. One-day news started spreading that Hoenstok would be leaving the team soon. In the meantime I had risen in the Dutch rankings. I was now playing in the second division and was also the only one to win my round recently against The Starter darts team. I pulverised my opponent. Piet Looijesteijn the captain of The Starter knew the Diplomats well. He arranged a test game in his bar to see if I was good enough to fill the vacant spot with the Winmau Diplomats. An opportunity like this was what every aspiring young dart player was dreaming of. Everybody, I mean everyone associated with darts wanted to play in that team. I stood there warming up, throwing arrows for an hour or two that evening, when out of the blue they called and cancelled. I was completely shattered. Totally heartbroken.

Raymond fighting his corner to land third place during the Super in Amsterdam.

The following Saturday I was relaxing at home when I got a call from Jan Brouwers. He was at the central station waiting to go to a darts match in Limburg. They were one man short and he asked me if I wanted to go with them and play for The Hague-A selection. In those days this invitation was just like an amateur footballer being invited to play for Ajax or PSV. For goodness sake, I hadn't even played for The Hague-B team yet. Obviously I couldn't possibly say 'no' to this offer. I remember smiling on the train, all the way to the match. To crown it all, I was named 'Man of the Match'. Frits Brummer and I both threw *a-hundred-and-eighty* during the game. At that time in Holland, this high score was still extremely rare. If you threw 3 triple twenties in one throw you were *The Man*. To put things in perspective, each team comprised of nine men. So in total 18 players took part that day and only 2 of them, only once, threw 180.

Some of us were playing a few hands of cards on the train on the way back, including Bert Vlaardingerbroek. It was there and then I heard from Bert that he was changing over to the Winmau Diplomats. 'That was going to be my place', I thought. However, it turned out to be a shrewd move. After choosing him to join them, for the following 6 or so years he became THE man to beat in The Netherlands. I became very disillusioned, thinking quite rightly, that I had not had a fair chance at showing them just what I was made of. They were supposed to come and check me out but had already chosen Bert.

The day after this, the Rotterdam Open was being held. Because I was so frustrated from this letdown, I felt that now more than ever, I wanted everyone to see just what I could do. I desperately wanted to win there…and I did. Later the Diplomat guys confided in me that perhaps they should have let me into the team at that point after all.

Raymond thinks of **Jan Brouwers** as the key person that helped him on his road to discovery. Jan taught Raymond all the tricks of the trade and tactics. Brouwers remarked: "As a young man I used to play darts in The Entertainer where Raymond played regularly with his friends. I saw quickly that he had a precocious talent; he had already developed much more skill than others of his age. He frequently threw around 100…140. Strange as it may seem now but back in those days this was not the norm. Now of course, good young players score at that level fairly consistently. At that time we only had a small number of youth players. Youth leagues were not even heard of here in The Netherlands, so I used to give him a game or two. That didn't work for him at all. He used to lose constantly and even then he was not a good loser. Raymond, still just around 17 at the time, did manage to beat me once and after that his appetite for playing seemed to grow by the day. He desperately wanted more.

I had to perform all kinds of dart manoeuvres and pull out all the stops, in order to keep him from beating me. It worked at first but increasingly became more and more difficult. I tried to break his concentration by walking slowly, playing faster or slower. These were tricks he still had to learn to overcome, things he could not handle. These methods of conjuring up a win just made him more upset. He became so frustrated with my darts antics, that he started kicking at things. He just had to find a way to beat me. When this started happening more and more, I eventually decided to ask his parents if I could take him along with me to tournaments. Fortunately for Raymond's dart career, they thought it was a good idea. The top 4 Dutch players were always at these meets. I taught him which players used which tricks. Then, straight out of the blocks in his first tournament he reached the last 16. I thought this was a fantastic achievement for a novice. I was extremely proud of him but Raymond, ever the perfectionist, was not so impressed by his own performance.

Jan Brouwers, "Amateur talent scout," a key figure in the discovery of Raymond the darts player. Jan taught him all the tricks of the trade and tactics.

He wanted more, more! At the next tournament outing, held in Breda, he got to the last eight, the quarterfinals. Then at only his fourth tournament, the Open in Rotterdam, he won! He played against Bert Bohemen in the final. I had to be at work at six that morning and he was still playing out the final at 1:30 am. That evening Raymond confided in me: 'Jan, I want to be world champion.' 'Yes Raymond,' I said, 'but the British are much better and stronger dart players than we are. It's their game after all, be realistic.' But he was adamant and so he continued his quest for stronger players to compete against and beat in The Netherlands. His game grew quickly, week by week even. Then he made another quantum leap by leaving these shores. In his thirst for experience and success, he started to travel abroad. Throwing down the darts gauntlet, challenging the rest of the darts world. After a temperate kick off, things started to go vertical. He went from strength to strength."

ieren

3ij de heren was er, ondanks het gemis ran de nodige topdarters, toch goed

Barneveld. In de andere halve finale was Ronald van Wensveen te sterk voor Jan Martens.

• *vlnr*
Raymond Barneveld
Ronald Wensveen
Jan Martens
zittend: Jan Brouwers

140-72, maar hij kon niet finishen en zo werd het 2-1 voor Ronald. De vierde leg was weer voor Jan: 2-2. In de beslissende vijfde leg ging het gelijk op. Jan wis eerder te finishen en won zo de partij

Om 21.00 uur konden de bekers worder uitgereikt. De organisatie was tevreder en hoopt op een succesvol vervolg als ir 1987 ter gelegenheid van het 5-jarig bestaan van de Venlose Darts Organisatie een heel weekend (wederom he derde weekend van september) word gedart.

Uitslag

Jeugd
1. Marcel van de Ven
2. Louis van Dissel
3. Will van Looy
4. Géke Smeets

Dames
1. Valerie Maytum
2. Ingrid Hulman
3. Carla Fleuren
4. Tineke van de Ven

Heren
1. Jan Brouwers
2. Ronald Wensveen
3. Raymond Barneveld
4. Jan Martens

Voor uitgebreide uitslagen zie Holland Darts Trofee.

A newspaper cutting from the mid-eighties. Raymond came third in this tournament, hosted by the Dutch Darts Magazine. Kneeling is Jan Brouwers, the guy who quickly discovered Raymond's latent talent for darts. A young Raymond is standing on the left.

Also according to **Rob**, Jan Brouwers was definitely the key person who initially discovered Ray and brought to light his darts crazy son's super talent. "Ray managed to make his breakthrough in darts when he was just 17, when Jan Brouwers discovered him. This was actually at the same time that I stopped being a carpenter and climbed into the lorry, so to speak. All of a sudden I wasn't able to be home every night. Raymond used to go to the café Het Valkennest on a Friday night in those days: 'I'm just going to earn my pocket money.' He announced. He played in the tournament and won Dfl 100. The following week he won again. Then I said to him, 'Why go there again? Why not go somewhere else this time?' He replied: 'I would be nuts. That would cost me a 100 guilders!' 'But what if you win, every week? Surely the rest of the boys at Het Valkennest won't want to play you anymore? You won't have any pocket money in two weeks time, if you keep going there.' He hadn't thought of that. Since that day Raymond always had a bit of extra cash in his pocket. He made a lot of new friends at the time but as to how many people turned out to be just friends with his money, you really don't want to know."

In 1984 I achieved my big breakthrough in Holland. They were good times, very exciting. At the end of that year I received an award for the most promising darts player. Michael van Gerwen was the same age when he made his more recent breakthrough: 17 years old. Jan Brouwers and his brother Hessel played for the The Hague-B selection. By playing a lot and pitting my darting wits against Jan, I was able to discover exactly where I had to polish up my game. I calculated, created and drew out a poster size scheme with all possible dart finishes imaginable and stuck it on the wall above my bed. All the options to throw out. Then I learnt them all off by heart! I discovered very soon that the obvious logical number sequences were not always that handy. For instance, to close from 75 in, you might easily fall into the trap of thinking that triple 15 and double 15 would be your best option. In fact it is not actually a very good choice. Because, if you throw a triple 15 and aiming at a double 15 accidentally throw a single 15, you are in trouble. Therefore, it is better to throw 75 using a different combination. For example triple 17, double 12. That way, if you miss the double 12 with your second dart, you always have an opportunity to hit the double 6 with your last dart of the throw. Jan taught me all these kind of ways to come out on top. A lot of this stuff was discussed while driving to all the Dutch tournaments in his Opel Kadett.

Down in Eindhoven I was named most promising darts player of the season. On the way home the prize, a special commemorative plate, was laying comfortably on the rear shelf of Jan's car. All of a sudden he had to break but still rammed the car in front that had stopped suddenly because of a traffic jam. Whaaack! 'Where is my plate, Jan, where's my plate?!' I shouted. While Jan just sat there brooding, leaning forward, looking over the bonnet surveying the damage. His vehicle turned out to be total loss...

Jan Brouwers also distinctly remembers the crash: "Almost straight after his triumph in Rotterdam he received another accolade in Eindhoven. We were on top of the world, both of us, driving home. One minute we were chatting casually, then all of an sudden the car in front of me stopped dead on the motorway. Unbelievable, by the time I saw what was happening, it was too late. We smashed straight into the back of it. My car was a complete write-off. The front of it was a total loss, we were lucky to get out in one piece and Ray's memorial plate went flying around the car.

'My plate, my plate where's my plate!' Raymond shrieked. 'Yes, yes... but what about my £$% car?' I replied.

The first time that Raymond stayed in a hotel in a foreign country was on his first trip to England. It was a laugh there. Late one evening back in their room his friend Dickie Pronk decided to have a shave for the first time in his life with a razor, for fun. Raymond explained to Dick that afterwards he had to put on a bit of aftershave. They had picked up a small sample of the stuff somewhere. So Dick innocently splashed it all over his freshly shaved skin, slapping it on gleefully with both hands! Disaster. He screamed out in instant pain. It was the middle of the night and the whole hotel was shaking as the noise was so loud. Ray always liked to have a bit of fun and joke around."

I used to buy my darts and accessories at the *House of Darts* on the Fahrenheitstraat in The Hague. The shop's not there any more now. These days there's *Darts World* on Almeloplein. I believe this new shop sprung originally from the *House of Darts*. You could also buy darts and extras at Vroom & Dreesmann or Perry Sport in the centre. That's where I bought my first set but now I always buy at a specialist outlet. Nowadays I always play with the same darts and flights, but in the beginning I just liked to play around with various materials, sizes, tips, shafts, weights, shapes of flights and so on."

Raymond's life was moving forward on two fronts because, as he started to play more and more darts, he still had to think about earning a living supporting himself. He had passed his final school exams and as darts didn't provide a steady income, he had to do some manual work. Working in the building industry for a living along side trying to build on his real passion, playing darts, was hard. Working in the construction industry was a big uphill climb for someone who was not that technically minded. In the end, both physically and mentally stumbling, Raymond called it a day and decided he was not cut out for construction work.

"After I had received my final school diploma I went along to the employment agency and they asked me what I wanted to do. Anything except carpentry. Apart from that statement I had no idea what I did want to do. Funny though, my first real job turned out to be technical, despite what I had said at the employment agency. It was a special project run by Heidemij, a Dutch construction company. Young men, straight out of school, were offered the opportunity to work with them on a so-called student project. There wasn't really much else available at the time, so I accepted. Five days a week, weekends free, hmm... I earned a meagre Dfl 694 per month and had to work 20 days or so every month.

My first project was to work on a house in the Koningsstraat. It had to be totally gutted inside and then completely reconstructed; a total inside renovation. I was sent in first to help with the demolition. There was another crew doing the actual reconstruction. Specialised guys. This part of the action would be too dangerous for someone like me to get involved in, the boss said. I managed to hurt myself anyway. I fell down two flights of stairs with a compressor in my hands. I picked that thing up, went off balance and fell straight down. Scaffold construction work is quite dangerous, you know. Also climbing up two or three flights of stairs carrying plasterboard and so on. Before you knew it, you could be lying at the bottom of the stairs again. After this particular fall with the compressor I had to have a couple of months off and ended up with a weak ankle for my troubles. I also managed to step on a sharp nail and even today, when it's cold and I walk around the house barefoot, it's still painful Once we were stapling plasterboards and the person I was working with started mucking about. He lost his concentration for a moment and… 'boom', he stapled right through his hand. I mumbled: 'Yes, hmm, well okay', while he was screaming with pain! We managed to pull the staple out right there and then. I realised very early on that I wouldn't be able to do this for the rest of my life, no way.

To compound this decision was the glaring fact that the risks attached to this kind of work did not match up well with throwing darts, which was becoming increasingly more important to me. Sawing, planeing, chiselling. No, I definitely needed to keep my throwing arm in one piece, thank you."

Two players that would go on to win the Dutch Open: Raymond van Barneveld and Jilles Vermaat, who also taught Raymond a lot.

Private Barney

After a very short, hardly successful manual labouring career, Raymond was then bound to be recruited into a whole new life. He was "Called-Up" for Dutch military service. Private Van Barneveld was sent to an Army Post in the East of The Netherlands, about 3 hours by car from The Hague, and he rather liked it. The fact that he had excellent hand-eye coordination was of course a bonus but above all his time in the army marked the start of a new social phase in his life. Friendship and camaraderie became very important to him.

"The project with Heidemij went on for a full year. After that I worked for the PTT, the Dutch Postal Service for a couple of months. I applied with Jan Brouwer's help, who had worked there for many years along with his brother. He said 'Just write an application letter.' So I did and got a job straight away as a postman, nice work really. I did my best and enjoyed it. I made Dfl 1,320 a month, nearly twice as much as previously. I worked in the office of one of the PPT buildings in The Hague on the Waldorpstraat, almost directly behind the Den Haag Holland Spoor train station. Unfortunately after a few months I was made redundant, as there were too many employees and not enough jobs. I was very unhappy and extremely upset I had to leave. I went straight back to the employment agency but they told me that, because in just a few more months time I would be serving in the military, no one would want to hire me now. So I received benefits for a couple of months until I went into the army. Not much of an income at all, but enough to help me through that vacant period. I was drafted into service when I was 20 years old. It was now 1987. I served for fourteen months, quartered at the Detmers barracks in Eefde, close to Deventer. I served with the light infantry, the 87-1 Guard Company. Boy, did we have some good times there! Guard duty was shared with the Americans for example. 'ReForGer' they were called, Rescue Forces of Germany. Every couple of years these Americans would come over to Europe for training. It was great. Good times in general. But… sometimes they were not so good. For example when I was called into duty, guarding nuclear warheads.

The duty began one Thursday morning at eight, and finished the next Thursday morning at around eight. It was only then, after a full week that I was relieved from duty. Stamina building, testing times, are not the phrases to use to describe this kind of situation. You really learn just how long 24 hours can stretch out in your mind. It seemed in the end like a week or more. Imagine yourself lying in a trench, looking out for the enemy who are not even there or likely to come there. After six hours you start going gaga, become a complete automaton. Staring at an empty road, hour after hour. It would have been half-bearable if there had been at least someone else there in the same situation but I was completely alone. All this for a whole bloody week!

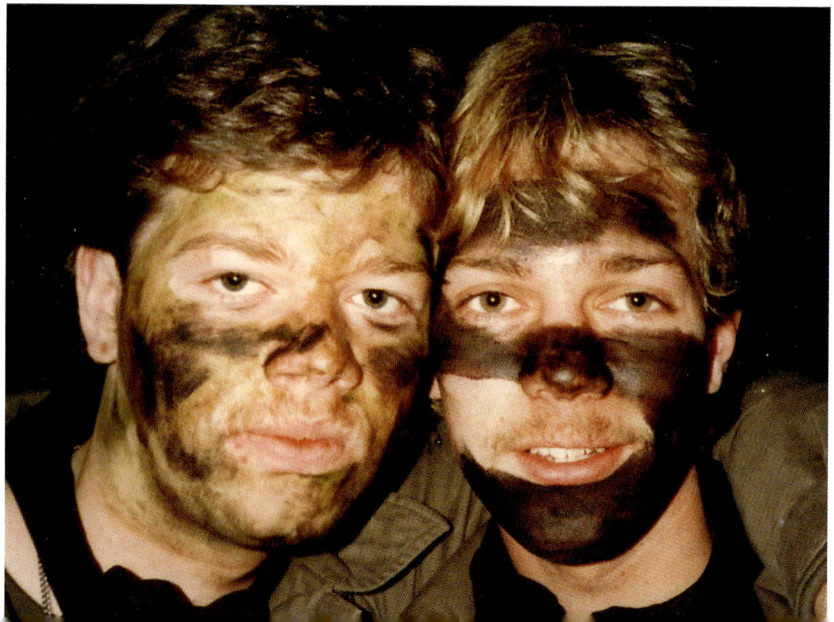

Raymond didn't feel like joining the army at all. Looking back it has made him very independent and he made some great friends there.

In military service the aiming skills I had developed from all my darts practice came in very handy. As it turned out, I was also good at aiming a firearm. I was a mean Uzi and FAL pistol sharpshooter. I covered the soldier who fired the rocket launcher, the Bazooka. I was also the only soldier in the platoon to have handled all the different weapons. The other soldiers usually only had FAL-rifles. This was the weapon that you started out with for the first two months. The rocket launcher was only armed with a pistol, so therefore needed extra protection and cover from another soldier in the platoon. I was the best shot around so I got the job. My personal weapon was an Uzi and I was the only one in my group who had one. Sharp shooting was one of my favourite activities but unfortunately we were not able to practise this very often. If you went shooting for the 'day' you were allowed to fire only about six times and that was it. There were so many safety measures in place. After you had fired a sergeant would come up to you, salute and ask if everything was okay. They also did all sorts of checks to make sure you were not 'pocketing', I mean stealing anything. No, you didn't practise on the shooting range very often at all, it was a pity that. Some other boys had told me that military service was like a fourteen-month long holiday but it wasn't like that for me. I was busy every day. I had to stay on the base the entire time. I couldn't travel back and forth home every day.

A couple of the guys I met and became friends with during my time in service, were Hans Boudesteijn and Peter Kool. Peter slept in the next bed to me in the barracks and I have stayed in touch with him. I have also kept in contact with Rob Jansen and Johan Imminga from Groningen from those days. They have sent me a few photos over the years. When I look at them I start thinking: 'Wow, guys, it's hard to come to terms with the years flying by.' Why does time pass by so quickly? Each time I receive a new photo everyone looks that bit older and maybe has had children etc.

We started with a group of about forty men but after just three months there were only 30 of us left, who served out the remainder of our duty.

I remember everyone was walking around moaning in the beginning: 'I wish that it was already next February, etc, etc.' Although, when it was eventually time to leave and go home we all started hugging each other. It got very emotional, we were even crying. After all the good and not so good times together, day and night, rain or shine, we had formed a bond. In the end it was very difficult to leave all that behind.

We were always mucking about! I remember once, we were riding in a three tonner – a very large truck. We were all sitting in the back as it was being driven along the motorway. Then a car came up right behind us with a hot young lady behind the steering wheel. A guy called Habets from our group made a well-known hand gesture at the woman. Then we branched off the highway, heading towards the barracks. Then, would you believe it, the woman did the same and followed us right into the compound. It turned out that this woman was the camp captain's wife. Yes, that event made for one embarrassed soldier's rapid transfer, obviously!

Exercise Minor War; this was something else. Three of us had to build a raft in the dark and it was pitch dark. The deal was no lights what so ever, otherwise the enemy would be able to spot us a mile off. Eventually we managed to start crossing the river IJssel, paddling through the water. Dark furry rats were swimming nonchalantly past, agh! We were only allowed to wear swimming trunks. After we reached the other side we had to get dressed again in the dark. So muggings ended up wearing some other bloke's socks, while he was wearing my helmet. Then I stepped straight into a heap of cow dung – yuk! So the moral of this story is: if in doubt and in a rush go for the socks first, not the helmet.

Eventually, I'm sure we would have done anything for each other. That's how thick we were together. We became extremely close. The experience kinda made me. Everyone says that, if you haven't already started beforehand, you're very likely to start drinking and gambling in the army. Believe me; I didn't start drinking until five years after I left the Army. It's quite well known that boys like to have a little flutter, a bet or two, in the army but I never saw any fun in this activity. I am not the sort of guy who would try to make a quick buck on the side from friends. Gambling does not do it for me. Yes, the card game 31 with a few coins thrown in the pot, maybe. No further than that though. Although I must honestly say that a poker tournament I took part in once on TV, was great fun. I enjoyed Texas Holdem but I think that was mainly due to it being an invitation event and you got to play with some famous people.

I made a few very good friends during my time in service. It seems a pity now though, looking back, that we didn't keep in touch and see each other anymore. This on the one hand I find quite surprising. Barney's email address can't be that difficult to find, can it? I must be easier to find than they are. Maybe not, so I joined a site called dienstmakkers.nl for Dutch service friends. Now I'm registered there, I have been able to make contact with some of the boys I served with. That's been great. Unfortunately I also found out that a roommate of mine passed away as a result of cancer. That made me feel very sad.

Raymond and his army pal Hans Boudesteyn.

The summer after I finished my service, 1988 it was, I went on holiday and while there thought I would send cards to the boys. I managed to send thirty in total. I got twenty replies back. The next year I sent twenty post-cards. As you only send to people who reply, don't you? This time I got five back and three years on I didn't even get one in return.

Having seen what I had been up to in the meantime they might have been be a bit cautious about replying. Maybe they thought: 'He probably won't have any time left over to be a mate like in the old days. Or maybe he doesn't really want to know us anymore. He's probably too busy and won't be sitting there waiting for our reply'. Well, if they did think that way, they could always phone and if I'm busy I would call them back.

Another thing I clearly remember from my service period, was being terrified of what they nicknamed the stereoprik, the stereo injection. You were given this simultaneously in both arms. Your arms would then start sagging, becoming quite heavy from the medical effects. Everyone complained about this stereo series, it hurt for ages, for weeks. Anyway…I still won a darts tournament that evening in the Cafe Het Valkennest on the Valkenboslaan in The Hague. I was terribly worried before hand, about the injection affecting my game but it turned out okay in the end.

The mandatory time I had to spend in service did put a bit of a dampener on my darting career though. I had to pass on some tournaments when they came along because I had duty, standing guard at the weekend for example. It wasn't easy to come to terms with these restrictions.

My father always used to tease me about having to go into military service. He said it would do me good. Maybe it would I thought but I really didn't want to go. In the end, when I look back, I realise that he was speaking wisely.The experience turned me into an independent young man. You know, when you are younger your bed is made for you and food is always on the table. Then all of a sudden you had to do it all yourself! I also made a lot of friends; we were all in the same boat. This was very good for me. I became an integral part of a great platoon there. We managed go out as a whole group too. It was a sort of whistle stop tour of the town of Eefde. Our first call was to the only snack bar in town, next to the only bar and then we had to return to barracks.

Because the TV reception on the camp consisted of only 3 stations we hired videos all the time. Our entertainment used to be drinking coke while watching these movies. Thinking back now, entertainment…was virtually non-existent. Fortunately there was the camaraderie, that great feeling of real friendship I had missed all those years without really realising it until this time. Yes, that made everything worthwhile. We also managed to 'Abscond' into Deventer once or twice, but this was only during the last six months of stay, as by then I had obtained my driving licence. So us boys could go out in the 'big city'.

There were a lot more girls around than locally which was great but I don't think I spoke to any of them. To tell you the truth I didn't dare. There were one or two girls who looked at me but I didn't return the signal. I still hadn't found the courage to do it at the time."

Raymond pictured playing Phil Taylor for the first time during the 1990 European Cup in Malta. Because of his good performance he was allowed to play at The Embassy.

The postman inhales his first Embassy

After his period of military service, Raymond would normally have had to look for civvy street work again. But he was a talented and fortunate boy, so before he had even closed out his service period he found work knocking at his door. Confident that he could now earn a living, his career took off once more.

"By chance two months before I was to be demobbed, I ran into Pieter Ratsma, the guy I worked with as a postman previously. I saw him delivering post along the busy Gedempte Burgwal. Then coincidentally he actually came right up to the door to deliver a package to the neighbour. We had a chat and he told me that they needed people at the post office. So I applied again and was accepted immediately. This time on a permanent basis, Yes!

I finished my time in service on the Friday and on Monday I was dispatched by the PTT, off on a two-week course. After this course I worked continually at the PTT on a permanent contract for nine years straight, from February '88 through to the end of '97. With not one day off work. I still liked the job and it was quite easy. That was except if there was a round where you had to call on the *Hoge Rijswijkseweg*, then you were not so lucky. You would have to deliver to the high numbers on the Rijswijkseweg, far away from the sorting office, carrying large packages from mail-order companies. Some people weren't in of course, so you had to write notifications and take the packets back with you all the way. Occasionally the bike might have a flat tyre but you still had to go on through the wind and rain blowing in off the North Sea. That bit was definitely not enjoyable. I must say on the other side of the coin though, on average I managed to get home from work every day at around one in the afternoon. Naturally, this was offset with a 6 am start but now I had loads of spare time and to boot, at one point I earned almost Dfl 3.000 net a month. The early bird call though, that was difficult, especially in the beginning but I didn't care too much as I was just glad to have a job at that stage. After a few years though, it did start to bother me. Doing a red-eye on a Saturday morning was not actually ideal, as I had usually played darts late into the evening the night before. Friday night could be a busy one at the dartboard. Twice a month the job demanded that I deliver mail on a Saturday. On top of that there were quite a few extra guilders to be earned doing someone else's Saturday shift for them. The money came in very handy but the extra day…to work a rolling six day week, was murder.

From the outset of my darts career I received a lot of support and backing from the PTT. I'm very grateful for this. They also sponsored me, giving me time off, etc. The PTT supervisors who generally took care of everything day to day were Erik Heslinga and Rob Verver. Rob has since, unfortunately, passed away. These guys really believed in me! They did what they did because they wanted to. Once I went to a meeting with them in their office and Rob, during the conversation turned towards me and asked: 'Raymond, how do you manage to do it?' He was referring of course to the fact that the newspapers often printed stuff like '…postman this' and 'PTT that…' Great adverts for the PTT. Yes, I would have loved to have been able to stop work, play darts full time and still receive a wage for sponsoring the PTT, say for another five years, just wearing that PTT shirt all the time. Unfortunately that little scheme had to stay in my head. Eventually I did get given three weeks extra paid leave per year and could also take unpaid leave. The need for Saturday work was fading fast and in the end I felt extremely fortunate when I heard I no longer had to work on a Saturday. Obviously I didn't earn the same wage as previously, but it was a great feeling not to have to get up at the crack of dawn at the weekend. However, my work colleagues were not over the moon about it at the time. Green-eyed looks had to be factored into the daily routine.

Military service was over and I was still young and single, so I could go out and do almost anything I wished now. In those days I often visited the Café *The Entertainer* or bowled along to a tournament with some of the local lads. There were lots of tournaments then. On a Friday evening there was a big tournament on at Café *'t Valkennest,* The Falcon's Nest on the Valkenboskade. The winner got to take home 175 *guilders*. Saturday would normally be reserved for playing in a Dutch national competition. Later in the evening I would go into the Coffee Shop called *Wout* on the Elandstraat, where I would play in another pub competition. On a Sunday it was either The Hague's Ranking event or a tournament organised by the *Dutch Darts Magazine* (HDM). The money I earned was a welcome bonus but I mostly played for fun, to practise and to promote my game. It was only later, when I was in a relationship, that I learned that money was more important than I had given it credit for in the past.

At the time I felt extremely honoured to be chosen to play for The Hague and later for The Netherlands and I still do. My darts career developed in a chequered way during this early period. Things did not always run smoothly. During this era there was a tri-country tournament running between France, Belgium and The Netherlands. Later this metamorphosed into The Spring Cup, producing an even bigger national rush of pride than the former. Belgium, who probably had a head start on France and us in The Netherlands, due to the earlier introduction of darts into their culture by the *Tommie's*, always won back in those days. This is the competition that I made my debut in when playing proudly for the Dutch team. There was an individual, doubles and team tournament, made up of four men in each team. It was a great experience and honour to win my place, qualifying me to play for the Dutch team. The win at the Rotterdam Open in 1984 meant that now everyone in The Netherlands, especially the darts world knew who I was. This meteoric rise however masked the fact that I wasn't any good at calculations.

This came to the surface a bit earlier when I was caught once during a game in The Hague. I was just 17 or 18 years old and playing a few set finishes with some other guys for fun. It was my turn with 75 remaining. They shouted out 17, then 18, which I duly bedded. Then came the order: 'Now double 15.' I promptly launched the last dart straight into the double 15. Fantastic, I thought. At that point they all collapsed laughing. What was the problem? Of course…I should have thrown for double top. Stupid! What a load of tossers! But I learnt from it, never to trust such calls again and am now prepared for anything in front of the board. The gang that was playing that night normally played in the G-Force and were real local tearaways. After that I took a few more lessons from Jan Brouwers and trained with him at his house on the Gagelplein."

Jan Brouwers noticed at that juncture already, that Raymond couldn't handle losing very well: "He took dart playing very seriously and so did not like losing at all. He had trouble handling it. He used to go ape sometimes, throwing things around and impaling his arrows into the ground. I had to call time-out, to give him a break and after a few minutes things flowed again. I must say that he was only mad with his own mistakes and himself, never pointing a finger, or dart come to that, at any one else. Naturally I thought at the time: 'Gee Wizz, what are you at, you're so young, and everyone's got to lose from time to time.'

Partly, because of this flaw and the potential I saw in him, I would try to help him with tips regarding tactics and concentration. Speed and precision has to come from within. If you know what a player is likely to do in advance, or work it out early in a match, you can anticipate his next move and pace yourself accordingly. Raymond has now learned a lot regarding these elements and styles of play. He has always had a problem playing slow players. But really, his world just seemed to implode, if he lost. These days he has matured a lot in his head. Back then he was too easily angered. His scoring memory has also improved. Previously, he could not subtract correctly. I still remember he lost once in The Netherlands Open, because of this. He was ahead in the semi-final. After two arrows he stood a good chance of closing out with 50 left to finish in the decisive leg. Now, instead of aiming for the bull and trying to finish there and then, he threw for an 18! This left him with 32, so double 16 to aim for in his next throw… But of course he didn't get a 'Next throw!' His opponent finished the game off within seconds. This incident in particular taught him a hard lesson about keeping mentally alert. Also about being composed and being one-step ahead in the counting game. He was so tense, he didn't notice the opportunity there in front of him, to bed in the bull. He never let that sort of thing happen to him again after that."

Raymond quickly learnt, that darts could mean much more in his life than just being a pastime he was very good at. Earning money was a great incentive, a motivator but being able to win consistently against so many different and varied types of opponents, gave him an even bigger thrill. He enjoyed his level already achieved and strived, constantly, to improve his game further. But as is the want, his first set-backs came from a most unexpected angle. They were psychologically based. Loose comments, made in envious asides from associates and dart players alike, magnified in his mind. He was being confronted by his most difficult opponent ever, himself. He had to learn extremely quickly one of the hardest of lessons in any professional sport, that winning does not just involve physical skill of the highest level. There is a winner's frame of mind that goes with the territory and is required to be developed as well.

"During 1988 I began to take part in some foreign tournaments. I went to the Belgian and German Open's. In those I ended up in third place a couple of times. It felt great to compete abroad. I then took part in the Swedish and the Danish Open afterwards, as a follow on. It didn't come cheap though. I had to pay for everything myself. On the up side, I had managed to win quite a bit of prize money in local tournaments by now. At the HDM-tournaments in The Netherlands I had become *the man*. However, this local fame and fortune didn't transmute through to my standing in the Dutch rankings, where I didn't fair that well at all. I kept going though, as I desperately wanted to seize the number one spot in The Netherlands and in the Dutch team. I was thinking too much, maybe too far ahead and consequently, didn't throw any good darts. I had to learn to keep my feet on the ground more. This struck me, when I realised that I didn't put myself under that much pressure while playing in the HDM games. Meaning I was doing much better in them, than in the national tournaments. When I was under pressure I often failed because I wanted to win too much, at all costs. This thought pattern was always my biggest downfall in the early days.

Unfortunately, in the meantime, the Post work slowly built up into drama level for me. I was moved sideways and in addition had to deliver unaddressed junk mail, three times a week. It was door-to-door work. When I started, there were four men working nightshift, sorting the mail for delivery the next morning. Then there were three, because of cutbacks and in the end only two had to do all that work. So of course when you arrived for work the following morning, the pre-sorting had not been completed or on worse days not done at all! That would normally take the first half an hour of my day shift to complete, before I even managed to get on the road. That's why I finished later and later in the afternoon. It wasn't much fun, not any more. Nowadays people start at seven, a full hour later than we did, in order to save TNT having to pay night shift premium.

I had an accident on my rounds, biking through my patch on 18 November 1988. I remember it well. I managed to fracture my wrist quite badly. I was pedalling on my PTT bike along the Saturnstraat close to the Ed Laurens cigarette factory. It was quite slippery from the early morning frost. I was just minding my own business, when …Whooosh the bike slipped from under me and I crashed down to the ground, crack, s**t. I just about managed to finish off my round and then went straight to the supervisor. He said: 'You'll be okay, it's doesn't seem that bad.' I thought otherwise so I managed to trade that afternoon's shift with a colleague. I did a deal, off-loading my post to him for 25 guilders and went straight to the hospital. After an x-ray I found out I had fractured the wrist of my playing arm! My hand was in plaster for two whole months! This of course meant that I missed out on all sorts of tournaments and I had just hit the top rankings in The Netherlands. More expletives I can assure you, followed. So much for my season. Remember I couldn't work either. I was pretty down for a long time it seemed. A truly awful period. I was left powerless. I just had to stand by and watch others winning all these juicy tournaments, with lots and lots of lovely lucre passing me by. In those days you also had the Van Nelle Masters. I had to call a no-show on that as well. I was as sick as the proverbial parrot. I was seeded so I was set to receive Dfl 500 starting money. In my youthful wisdom I assumed that I would still receive the guaranteed money. But oh no, it went on a detour, straight to my replacement. This made me furious at the time. If I had known, I would have turned up and played left handed."

The organization probably wouldn't have allowed him to do this. Raymond just had to get on with life, the same way that every other person with a fractured wrist would have to, just be patient and wait for it to heal. In this case his enforced patience and fired up *I'll be back* mentality was rewarded in the end. No, it wasn't the first time that he had managed to turn setback into achievement and yes, within the first few games of his return he was reinstated into the Dutch darts team.

"It was in 1991 that I was invited to take part in my first Embassy. I heard the news during the European Cup played out in Malta. There, with the Dutch team, we all played quite well. I reached the last eight, the quarterfinals and guess who turned out to be my next opponent? My future greatest rival, the one and only Phil Taylor. *The Power* himself. In the end I lost 4-2, missing four close out arrows that would have brought me level at 3-3. There was a silver lining though. Olly Croft and Sam Hawkins from the British Darts Organisation (BDO) happened to be sitting there, watching the competition. Bert Vlaardingerbroek had already been invited three times to compete in their prestigious tournament, without making any great impact as such. So they were on the look out for some fresh new Dutch blood to enter their midst. After seeing my performance they decided that they would give me a chance by handing me a wild card, allowing entry into the prestigious UK Embassy. The news came via our national coach Gerard Beekmans. He came up to me quietly and announced quite bluntly and in a matter of fact way that I had been chosen to participate in *The Embassy*. I replied excitedly: 'Yes, I might even win and qualify for *The Embassy* itself.' Then he explained the deal slowly in more detail again and again, repeating himself about five times, before it sunk in. I was being allowed a free ride, posted straight into the main tournament. For a moment or two I was dumbstruck. It seemed a dream come true at last. But the dream quickly turned into a nightmare on the stage.

The moment arrived and together with Beekmans we left for *The Embassy* tournament. I drove to Utrecht and picked him up in the car, then we drove to the Hoek and caught the ferry to Harwich. We stayed in Frimley Green for the entire week. Gerard had taken extended leave, as he also wanted to enjoy the Lakeside Country Club's atmosphere for a while. I played my opening game of the tournament on the first Saturday evening. It was the first round proper and I lost 3-0 to Keith Sullivan from Australia. It was a K.O. competition and so elimination was immediately. A few weeks earlier, he had come home third in the British Open, so the warning signs were there. I heard that he had trained with Bob Anderson for an entire month prior to this event. This gave him a head start. I don't mean to say this as an excuse for losing, that I would have stood a better chance if things were different. No, not at all. It was an overwhelming occasion for me and my main problem was, that I was extremely nervous.

If I'm honest I was caught in a sort of ego trip. I was more worried about how I was being perceived and how I looked, rather than with my darts performance. I was in a sort of daze of wonderment, mainly looking around taking in the atmosphere, the crowd, the noise and the hype. So I wasn't focused on the game at all well. As far as I can remember I did win two legs in the second set but that was the highlight of a weak performance by my standards. As an after thought, I was extremely pleased with the fact that the match was not broadcast live on BBC TV. Meaning that no one in The Netherlands would have seen my display or lack of it. I did however manage to bring myself to watch the Sports news that evening. After all it was going to be my first appearance on T.V. wasn't it? But after all that, they only broadcasted the results. I didn't come to much that year. I was stiff as a plank and full of jangling nerves during that game. We mustn't forget that Bert Vlaardingerbroek was definitely the best Dutch dart player of that era. Everyone around seemed to feel that he should have gone there to fly the flag for Holland. On his first visit to *The Embassy* he had thrown very well, competing against Bob Anderson. In fact Bert was the only one, up until the final, who was able to take a set off of Bob. Before I even left The Netherlands I already heard background commentary about this upcoming tournament: How is he going to cope over there, etc., etc. This stuff kept going round and round in my head on the day. I didn't even drink a drop of alcohol and settled on lots of water instead but that didn't help either.

It was not a happy time, being there. Nowadays you have iPods or DVD's and the like. Then you didn't have anything like that in the way of personal entertainment. Back in your hotel room there was BBC 1 and BBC 2 and that was it. I didn't know anyone there either of course. Back then all the great names hung out together and

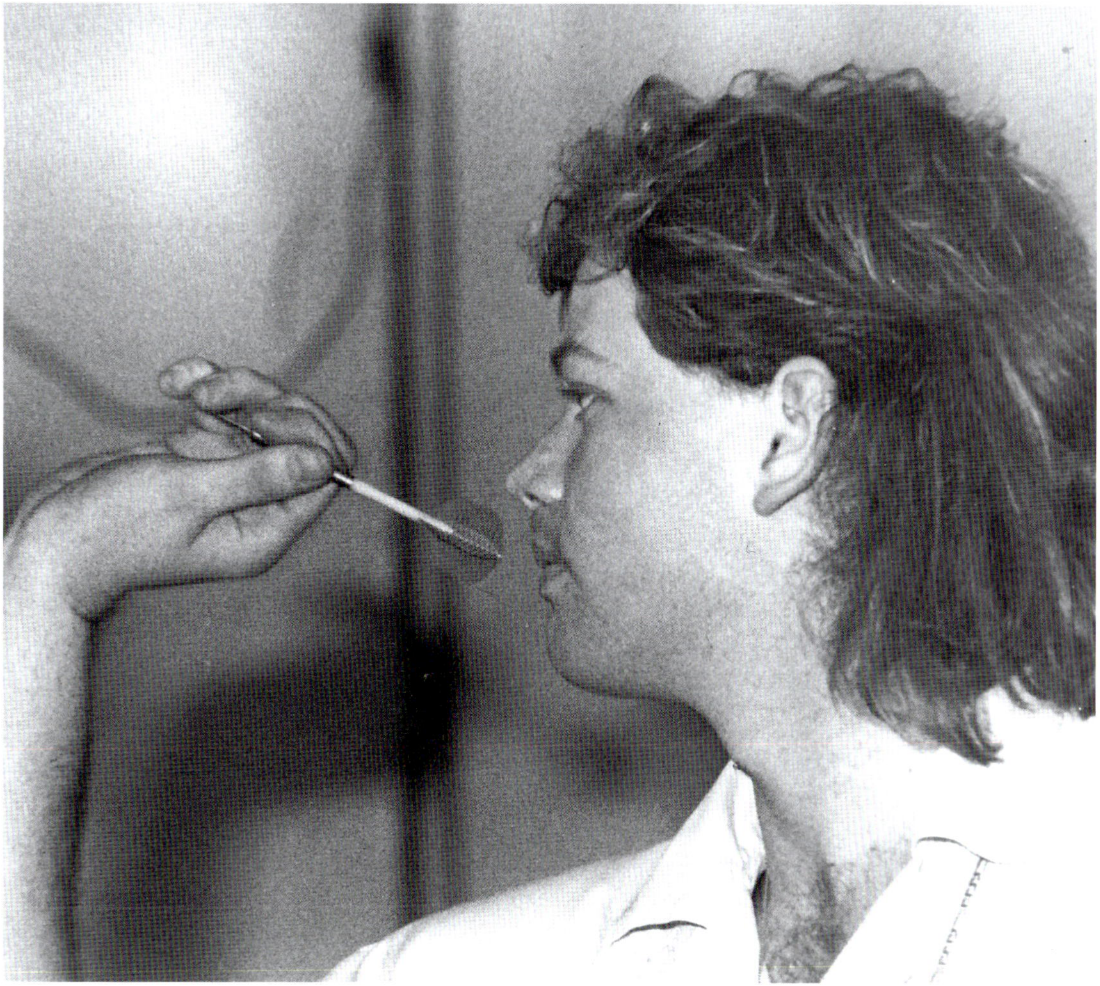

Raymond played The Embassy for the first time in 1991. Young and fresh but naïve to the surroundings, he was wiped out in the first round. This early defeat led to him not being selected to participate the following year but this did not deter him. He continued to practise and practise undauntingly.

nobody had much time for a new boy on the block from where, The Netherlands? I must say there were a few other new boys around as well. A Norwegian, a Belgian and a Dane. The four of us were all sort of in the same boat together. It did turn out for the good in the end, because I was still able to take part in the social side, the banquet and so on. So I smiled ruefully to myself that at least I would know now what to do, if ever I made it to *The Embassy* again. But this whimsical thought was quickly overruled with the overwhelming feeling that this was never, ever, likely to happen. I returned home, tail between legs, with the impression that I had said my last farewells to *The Embassy*. I didn't think I would ever receive another invite.

Obviously on my return home there were questions, questions, questions flying around from here, there and everywhere. It would be an major understatement to say that it was not a very good time for me. The experience definitely made a big dent in my confidence. The BDO officials said kindly: 'We will have to wait until next year then', but I didn't go for that in my heart. Even worse: The whole episode quickly turned into an epically frustrating period. Later in the year I played in the WK, the World Championship, in Zandvoort and lost in the second round to a Fin, who in turn beat Phil Taylor in the next round. I had underachieved big time but Bert Vlaardingerbroek had been outstanding there!

So the inevitable outcome was, that Bert was selected for the upcoming Embassy again. He was given another chance. He played in that 1992 Embassy against Welshman Martin Philips in the first round. Bert went into a 2-0 lead, but eventually lost 3-2 in a best of 5 sets."

Left: Bert Vlaardingerbroek still proved to be the best Dutch dart player around in the late eighties and early nineties, without a doubt. Middle: The best Britisch female dart player from those days, Valerie Maytum.

Silvia and Raymond, pictured together for the first time, at her parents home. Head over heels in love.

Love

Despite his two defeats at The Embassy and the WK in Zandvoort, things in general kept getting better for him within the national league darts world. Raymond earned a lot on the local circuit. But where were the girls in his life? Eventually, in spite of his shyness, he met someone and they fell in love. This also proved to be of great joy to his sister Bianca. Not necessarily because of her feelings for her brother but as this meant he would now vacate his attic room. She moved straight into the spacious room of Raymond's, only days after he moved out. The relationship however didn't last, so it wasn't too long before Raymond moved back home. Now he had the bug though, so off he went again not so long afterwards.

"I haven't had many girlfriends in my life. My first real girlfriend lived in Leiden. I was already 22 but I don't think I had ever been in love before then. So how did I hook up with her? I have never been the type of guy to make the first step in a relationship and say: 'I love you.' I have always been shy about love and even now I am still as shy as I used to be then. I lived with Natasja, my first real girlfriend, in Leiden for a year. I don't think I can even remember now how my parents reacted when I told them we were going to become an item and live together. My sister Bianca was overjoyed, because she got to move into my old attic room!

I remember my father was not very happy. He had difficulty accepting it and I had not anticipated that reaction from him. I thought that my mother might have found it difficult, but it turned out that she was more laid back than dad. She was just happy to have some peace and quiet in the house for a change. It was probably quite a relief for her, less to worry about. Personally I found it to be pretty challenging but also rather exciting. For the first time in my life I had to pay the bills myself. As opposed to when I lived with my parents. Then I only had to pay some money towards the general bills and that wasn't much. Now all of a sudden, I had to do things like pay the rent and all the other regular expenses. Fortunately I have always had a fair sense of responsibility. I have never thought of spending more than I earnt, so I coped quite well I thought. Our relationship didn't last in the end. Natasja and I felt that it was not going anywhere. We decided to end the relationship, go our own ways, parting amicably.

Rob: "When Raymond left home I was quite concerned. Not because I wanted to keep him home I mean but because I was not sure if he would be able to stand on his own two feet yet. Bianca moved into his attic-bedroom and I turned her bedroom into a hobby room. When Raymond and Bianca broke up he moved back in there, together with three cats! I said to him 'Look, you can sleep in the hobby room for the time being, just while you are looking for another place to live, okay.' Not long after that, he met Silvia.

I know Raymond inside out. He told her the story that he had to sleep in the train room and before we knew it, he was off again. In the past Raymond had always paid his way, living at home. But because he was starting over, we didn't ask it of him this time. When he was still struggling to keep his relationship alive with Natasja, he came home once with shoes, a handbag, jeans, perfume and some other things that he had bought for her from his winnings at a tournament. He hadn't thought to buy anything for his mother, who just had to sit and watch, as he handed out all these gifts in the living room. The following morning I took him aside and said: 'We need to talk son. When we told you that you didn't have to contribute towards the house keeping, we thought you were going to save the money to get back on your feet again but if you are going to spend it all on trying to win your girlfriend back, then you better start paying for your lodgings again.' That statement, along with the fact that he had to sleep in the hobby room was the deciding factor that motivated him to leave for the second time in a few months. He was off and for a while after that, we barely had any contact at all."

Regarding girlfriends, I've actually only had two, Natasja and Silvia. With Silvia it was a different set of circumstances than previously. I was older then, around 25 years old. I was a lot more experienced in the ways of the world than before. Fate had it that both of us had a failed relationship in our past. Yea, finally a mutual topic of discussion! I had fancied her for a long time, but in the beginning she had a steady boyfriend. A few years before, I was always saying to my former brother in law, Rob den Toom:'You know that Silvia, she's great.'

I hadn't seen or heard from Silvia for years. Then one day when we were in The Entertainer and I was playing a darts tournament, Rob mentioned: 'By the way your favourite girl is single again. Her boyfriend has left her and she is on her own, looking after her two children.' The news prompted me to go to the Concurrent in Maas Street where she worked, to try and have a word with her, the following Monday evening. Silvia was there, helping behind the counter but at that point I didn't know that she was also attracted to me.

It was easy to start up a conversation because not so long ago she had asked me for my autograph. I still remember what I said to her that evening: 'Will you be looking to go out with anyone again?' She replied: 'Not if I don't like the look of them.' I backed off immediately. Just as I had managed to pluck up all my courage!

A few more weeks passed before I decided to play some darts at the Concurrent with Hans Spaans, a colleague from the Post. Silvia was behind the counter that time as well. As the evening went by and we got talking, we realised that we were getting on really well together. So the following Saturday night we went to see a film. *Home Alone*, was the film I chose!

Before we went I was put through the 3rd degree, being introduced to her family. First we were only going to see her grandfather, I thought, who lived on the Maasstraat 98. When we got there, her whole family had turned up as well! With a big lump in my throat I croaked: 'Hello, I am Raymond...' Some people I already knew, like her uncles, as I had met them while they wereworking alongside my father. They were carpenters. Later, after the film, we went and had some drinks and then smooched and kissed for the first time. It was early December 1992.

A month later my name was to be seen again in *The Embassy* programme, for the year 1993. I went with the now retired Dutch national coach Rob Samuels and Jacques Nieuwlaat*. The reason I was invited again was because I had played a lot of international tournaments recently and collected enough points to qualify, based on my present position in the world rankings. I headed for England again with joy and optimism in my heart. I was also helplessly and hopelessly in love. That wonderful sensation helped me feel completely relaxed as I was throwing. No worries, I thought, if I lose I'll just pack up and go back home to my new girlfriend. Actually I didn't even want to leave her in the first place. I was really smitten. That year I became the first Dutchman ever to make it to the second round. I think I wanted to show everyone they had been wrong not to let me return the year before, in 1992, when Bert was invited instead of me. Motivation, motivation, motivation.

* Footnote from the writers: Jacques Nieuwlaat is a dart player originating from the very early days that the sport became popular in The Netherlands. He is also an SBS 6 Dutch TV commentator for big dart tournaments, as well as a presenter of dart galas.

Barney in June 1992, during a competition.

In that first round tie of the '93 Embassy I managed to beat Graham Miller 3-2. A year earlier Miller had made it to the last four, losing to John Lowe 4-3. Thus, the newspapers had called him 'spoiler', someone who could spoil the rankings and perhaps go unusually far in the competition. I remember, just before our game, Miller stood at the side of the stage discussing which of the two shirts he had, he should wear when he faced-up to me. Purely using a bit of *Haagsche Bluf*, I said that blue suited him better and it wouldn't matter too much, because I wouldn't give him a chance to wear the red one anyway. He seemed taken aback by the remark to the extent, that I felt it affected his game. He didn't play very well that day. Through these formative dart-playing years I did learn to speak up for myself. Also around this point I had started to enjoy downing a few drinks and this gave me an added boost of courage. It was already turning into a great match and competition. I threw 164 to finish the game. Yes, I was through to the second round. Unfortunately at that stage I lost 3-2 to the eventual champion of that year, John Lowe. He beat Bobby George in the final 5-3. However, to my great pleasure, I managed to complete two fantastic finishes during the tie from 161, and 170. I was just feeling on top of the world and... Anyway, I had nothing to lose, did I? I did know deep down though, that beating Lowe would probably be a bridge to far. So I was pleasantly surprised when at the end of the game, despite the fact that I lost, I received a standing ovation from the mainly British audience for my performance. It was a great moment for me. I 'm very proud that I was able to play against some of the best players in the world, before the split with the PDC came about. This Embassy stood out as a great success compared with my debut 2 years beforehand. I had now been able to show the darts world that I could hold my own, stand my ground against the very best.

The journey back home on the Harwich-Hoek ferry felt like a twenty-four hour trip, rather than the actual eight it took. I was desperate to see Silvia as soon as possible. Then, as we arrived at the quay-side, I saw Jacques, who had gone back earlier with his girlfriend Bianca, my dear friend Albert Vroegop and Silvia waiting and waving to me, as the boat docked. Magic!"

His success at the '93 Embassy was a turning point, a watershed. It changed his life in many different ways. Raymond had already made a name for himself in The Netherlands. His private life had recently been turned upside down and then righted again. He had catapulted from being a single man, on through a failed relationship, to finally falling desperately in love. On top of that he had become an almost instant father to two children. Not an easy task. It required a steady and adult mind-set.

"I knew from the onset of our relationship that Silvia had children. It was never an issue for me. Mike was 3 then and Daisy 6 months. The thing I did find difficult was having to explain things to my parents. How would they react, I wondered? All of a sudden their son had found a new girlfriend and two kids. Very gently and cautiously, I explained the facts. 'Mum and dad, I have met a woman who I think is wonderful... and she has two children.' Fortunately my parents saw everything in a positive light. They also insisted that I invite Silvia for Christmas. That's how it started. Mike came with us but we felt that Daisy was still too small. For the first year she was raised mainly by my in-laws. Silvia was going through a terrible time after her relationship with Marcel broke up. However, I like to think we managed to help her get through a lot. Winning the occasional tournament was a bonus. With some of the winnings I went out one day and bought a baby-stroller for the little girl. Silvia broke down in tears there and then. She said it was because I was being so kind to her and Daisy. I adjusted into the father role immediately. In the blink of an eye, I had become a dad with two small children. Boom, just like that. I must say all in all, it wasn't a walk in the park. It took a while to get used to the whole situation. I had to transform from a young and carefree single man, to the head of a family, in a matter of weeks. Before this of course, I was free to do what I wished. I would go out most nights and do whatever. I'm pleased to say that I managed to adjust and it all worked out well in the end.

My darts career was starting to become a bit like The Cony Island Cyclone though. It seemed that after every high, a big dip would follow. Wanting to build on my success at the '93 Embassy, I was looking forward to competing again in '94 but then came the disappointment. I wasn't chosen for the 1994 tournament! Still being number one in The Netherlands though, I was allowed to participate in the pre-tournament qualification rounds. Unfortunately I lost to the Scot, Trevor Nurse, in the final. So I didn't qualify but they still wanted a Dutchman to compete in the tournament. Eventually they homed in on Roland Scholten who had won the World Cup in Las Vegas in 1993. He was invited."

The Embassy in those days was the only tournament that was aired on the television and also where it was possible to earn substantial prize money. Raymond was banking on being able to enter the tournament and was quite unhappy he couldn't cut-it that year. For him this early K.O. meant yet another year of PTT postal rounds and chasing prizes on offer around the international circuit, in order to complement his day job. There were no long-term doubts in his mind though. He was still determined to make it to the top and quietly knew that he had it in himself to do just that.

"In February 1994 our daughter Patty was born. At the time we were able to laugh about the one big advantage we had. There were already lots of small children in our family, so finding clothes for her was no problem at all. I must say, that we didn't have a lot of money, when we started out together. At the time I was earning around Dfl 2.500 a month, with the PTT. In those days that level of pay was not too bad but with three children in the nest, it didn't go very far. First there was the rent of Dfl 800 a month, then the gas and electricity bill and on top of that we needed Dfl 300 for groceries every week. For a family our size that was not too excessive. With nappies, wipes and baby food, the minimum amount the shopping bill started off at each week was Dfl 60 and went up from there.

Additionally I didn't have a sponsor, except myself. I had to pay for all my dart trips out of my own pocket. Later sponsors became interested in me, but until that point it was a real struggle. I was coming out at Dfl 1,500 short every month! I managed to fill this gap by winning a dart tournament every now and again. In the end it got to the point where I felt that I was trying to win purely from a will to survive financially. I was desperately struggling to make ends meet. Silvia of course, had her hands full at the time with the children, so couldn't work either.

We never managed to go on vacation during those first few years. We just never had enough money to go round. When I received my holiday pay of Dfl 1.500 we knew instantly that it was not enough to enable us to go on holiday together with the three children. It was very frustrating. All the money that I managed to save was needed for repairs and so on. But, don't get me wrong: I always seemed to be able to come up with a guilder or two, quite amazingly. I didn't once have a problem paying the rent. Well, maybe once but I could have managed myself in the end. Tobie van Laarhoven wanted me to be able go to the 1998 Embassy without any worries on my shoulders, so he just gave me Dfl 1.500. Wonderful man! Because of this gesture, I was void of worry when I entered the competition. One month later, bingo, I was crowned world champion. Tobie van Laarhoven and Marco Hesselberth had unquestioning belief in me and carried that belief on to thinking I had the world title almost in my grasp. At the time their support had built up to the point where they always financed my international trips and never asked anything in return. It's thanks to these two benefactors, Tobie and Marco that I was able to develop as a professional dart-player. This kind of backing was pretty rare back then. As the years march on I have often reflected as to just why they spent their hard-earned money on supporting me, incredible guys. They must have poured in thousands and thousands of guilders between the two of them over time. I questioned them once about their generosity and they replied to the effect that they just liked me as a friend and knew that I had it in me to prove them right. To this day I'm very indebted to them both for the part they have played in my darting career and I'm thankful I did manage to make it, with their support."

Tobie van Laarhoven ran a chimney sweeping company in Den Bosch, in the south east of The Netherlands. He spotted Raymond's potential very early on. He supported him financially and psychologically. "It was a strange combination of events that led to us meeting. By a series of chance encounters I ended up becoming friends with some figures in the Dutch darting world. I was eventually introduced personally to Raymond through a fellow dart player, Braulio Roncero. I had spoken briefly to Raymond once before in Someren. He had just curtly instructed a child to move out of his way, so he could throw. Not very nice eh? I found this quite authoritarian and told him so. I can still picture him there. Raymond can't recall this incident anymore, but I can.

One year Braulio invited me to his hotel in England. The whole Dutch team was staying there, including Raymond. At first I did not take to the idea of meeting him because of what happened in Someren but Braulio persuaded me. It turned out to be a great evening. I got to know Raymond in a way I wouldn't have previously imagined. We ended up laughing and joking together the whole evening. He also explained why he had acted the way he did, in Someren. It was not because he didn't like kids. No, he was just under a lot of pressure, because he didn't have a lot of money. He said that he had to go for every tournament and had to win every time. Otherwise the expenses he needed for his next one, wouldn't be there. I was sympathetic and mentioned that, if he wished, we could discuss the subject again, another time, in private. I immediately felt I wanted to help him financially. In the end he let me and so I did help him out from time to time.

It was at the Gesloten Nederland tournament in 1995 that our agreement came to life. I was there as a spectator and Raymond spotted me, walked over and asked if I still remembered him. 'Of course', I replied. 'Do you also remember that we discussed my financial situation, a while ago in England?' He reminded me a little more and consequently, I made him a proposal there and then. I made my intentions very clear. I was to be his mentor, as well as a benefactor. He had no problem with either. As long as he could play his darts without the constant financial worries, he was a happy man. That's it, that's how our darting alliance was initiated. Apart from the small amounts of money that I used to sponsor him with, I was also able to guide him with his career. A strong mutual friendship developed from the outset. We used it to help and support each other, both in good times and difficult ones.

I predicted at the outset of our liaison that Raymond would, within five years, be the number one darts player in the world. He thought this was very funny at the time. When he did win *The Embassy* in 1998, the first thing I said to him was: 'Raymond why is it you can never stick to what we agreed? Not even today? I thought we said it would take you five years to win this.' We both roared with laughter.

We still keep in touch by phone every week, even now. The time came though, that in order to make sure he could continue to grow further, I had to let things take their natural course, rather than just promote my vision in particular. So I did. It wasn't easy but it was the best thing to do. The memories are wonderful and for a fair few years we went through a lot of action together. These kind of relationships are priceless and brought us very close as friends. The fact that we are still regularly in touch, is testament to our sincerity towards one another."

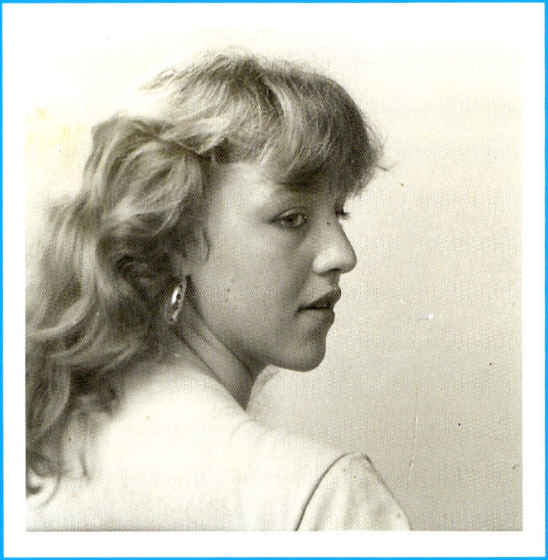

Silvia about her youth and Raymond

Before Silvia Walraven met Raymond in the autumn of 1992 she had already led quite a colourful life. Just before they first met, she stood one day on the steps of her parent's house, very pregnant, clutching the hand of her 3-year-old son. Just gazing out, focused nowhere, feeling miserable. She was on her own with the thought of two small children to feed, cloth and nurture. Because of a failed relationship, she had forgone everything, except the clothes she was wearing.

Silvia was born and bred in The Hague. On the 4th of September 1965 to be exact, at her parent's home on the Maasstraat. She had a very happy childhood. Silvia explained further: "My parents always knew if I was up to something in those days. We lived in a pleasant, close-knit neighbourhood. Everyone was welcome into everybody else's house. It seems that people lived more for each other in those days. We would sometimes get some biscuits from the neighbour, or run over there if there were unexpected visitors and you had nothing in the house to drink. Great, I liked that atmosphere but when people passed away, it was terrible. Suddenly, aunt Saar who used to walk her dog past the house every day, didn't come by anymore. She always had a sweet hidden somewhere in her bag for me, I remember that. These people were missed, even if you were only a child at the time."

Silvia went to the Roodkapje (Little Red Riding Hood) nursery school on the Scheldestraat. After leaving the nursery she went on to the Jan van Nassau School where, later, her own children also went to school. "I was a bit of a dreamer in the beginning. If I heard a word, especially a new word, I would sit thinking, with my hand under my chin, fantasising about the word and its meaning, creating countless stories out of nothing. I was also terribly afraid, that if I did something wrong in class, a teacher or the children would laugh at me. I still have this fear but fortunately now I know how to handle it much better. It was only after I reached year 6 at school, now called year 8, that I dared to speak up at all. To complicate matters further my handwriting was terrible and I was acutely aware of the fact. After leaving primary school I didn't really know in what direction I wanted to go. So, when I was 13 years old, as that's when you move schools in The Netherlands, I moved on to the domestic science and housekeeping school, situated on the Wilhelminastraat, in The Hague. It was a 4-year course, but every time exams came up I was overcome with fear. It was terrible. The day of the exams I would wake up in the morning with a high fever. What was I to do? In the end I decided to leave. It all became too much of an ordeal. I was just 16 when I came home one day and blurted out to my parents that I wouldn't be going to school any more, that was it. Fortunately my parents said that in the end it was up to me to decide. They knew that school was not really for me. So there I was, no school but also no work! 'You will have to go to work now though, you know', they said, although they probably would have been happier, had I stayed on at school for a bit longer. My sister had left school already and had an office job with the Insurance Company, AEGON.

I imagined that I had things pretty much worked out. I thought I would be able to put my feet up and relax at home, no problem. Not so, I hadn't even been at home for a couple of days, when my father said: 'So young lady, what's happening next? When are you going to go out to work?' My father was firm in that way. He couldn't work anymore himself, although he really wanted to."

Silvia's first job was working in the Dr. Van de Hoog Cosmetics factory. She only managed to stay at home for one week, following the abrupt ending of her school career. She worked there happily for three years solid. Then she moved away from The Hague, having found herself a partner who lived in Rotterdam. "I met Pim Steenhouwer, while staying on the campsite in Hattem. He worked there. I fell hopelessly in love from the word go! After a while we started living together. We lived quite close to the Sophia *Kinderziekenhuis*, the Children's Hospital in

Rotterdam. Raymond met him too, as Pim was also a darts player. Once we had settled in down there, I worked in a coffee shop and at the flower market. The hours were, six in the morning until two in the afternoon. When I got fed up with it, I started working in the abattoir. I worked there six days a week, full on. That was until I was accused of pocketing Dfl 93 one day. I guess it didn't dawn on my boss to look closer to home. His son was a junkie and had, coincidentally, just been released from prison! I was not going to stand for being wrongfully accused so, at six in the morning, I packed my things, took the money that I was owed out of the till and left. When I started going out to work I never took any sick leave and always worked very hard. Sick leave? My philosophy is if you don't have a fever you are still able to work. After all no-one has ever died from working when being a bit poorly, have they, now."

From left to right: Silvia, cousin Jacqueline, her mother and sister Ria.

The ending of the relationship with Pim was difficult. "He was my first serious boyfriend. When I realised he was not the one for me, it was very difficult to leave. You see, he had a grandmother, a wonderful woman who was very ill at the time with lung cancer. There she was, lying in hospital, dying and I wanted to talk to him about ending our relationship? You know, I just couldn't do it. It was definitely not the right time. Eventually I did mange to pluck up courage however and end it. I remember it was just before I was supposed to go on vacation to Spain, with Pim's other grandmother. I must admit that by then, I had already fallen in love with someone else. I left our place in Rotterdam with just my clothes. Nothing else! I was, after all the one who left, wasn't I? I even left the washing machine and the linen set my parents gave me. Mind you in the end they gave me these presents three times!"

Silvia was back home with mum and dad again! This time she lived there for a relatively short period, only two months. "Get everything back in order before you start off again on some new venture. You see, I was brought up to be open and honest. My mother taught me that: 'Everyone tends to tell a few white lies occasionally, but at least try to be as honest as possible. If you're not able to, best say nothing.' Together with: 'You may get away with eating with your hands when you're at home but make sure that you know how to behave when you're out."

Silvia threw herself into her next relationship with Marcel Batelaan completely: "He lived on the Vreeswijkstraat in The Hague when I moved in with him. Marcel was exactly six months older than me. We slept in one cot, side by side, when we were babies, because my mother used to clean at the same place where his mother worked. Marcel was a non-identical twin. Strangely his sister was going to be named Silvia too but unfortunately she died at birth. This fact formed a very emotional bond between us both. I had already known Marcel for quite a long time beforehand. Also from socialising around darts events. It was not long after we started going out that we bought a small house on the Zandvoortstraat in Scheveningen."

Mike their son was born in the Autumn of '89. "Shortly after this we went for a week's holiday to Zandvoort, mainly because The WK darts was being played there at the time. I collected autographs of the players by asking them to sign the competition programme. This included a certain Raymond van Barneveld. He seemed very shy and did not say much when I asked him for his signature. I did hear at the time from some other people, that he had a bit of a crush on me but I was in a relationship and had just had a baby, so I didn't give it a second thought. My sister and brother-in-law knew him well from the darts circuit. My sister also played darts, in fact, the whole family did come to think of it. It wasn't the first time I'd bumped into Raymond. I first met him while camping in Hattem. I happened to go and watch a darts tournament in the area. I was 17 years old and had never spoken a word to Raymond prior to that. In those days, he was a skinny kind of guy with long hair.

I was 24 when Mike was born. His birth was unexpected but welcome, nevertheless. The first test I took was a big YES, saying that I was pregnant. 'It's positive', the Doctor's assistant who helped me, said. 'Oh great,' I thought with relief, and replied: 'thank you.' But later it seemed she meant that I was pregnant, not that I wasn't. However since then we adjusted to the situation and having Mike turned out well. He was a wonderful child, right from the day he was born."

In the end the relationship with Marcel lasted five and a half years, all in all. Silvia was already pregnant with her daughter Daisy, when the relationship broke up. "With a child in my arms and a second one on the way I was standing on my parent's door step, once again! Fortunately they received me back with open arms. I slept with Mike in the attic. It was all very emotional at the time of course. In fact it was a very difficult time for us all. In the first 6 weeks alone I lost 26 kilos in weight! Daisy was still only six weeks old when I started seeing Raymond. He never made any fuss of the fact that I had two children. It wasn't an issue at all. Raymond always made himself available for our new family and was very understanding with the whole situation. Mike and Daisy have always been allowed to see their biological father. We have maintained from the beginning that the children should always be able to see their father.If you don't, you only end up distressing the father and the child. I have seen many men cry because they hadn't been able to see their children for years. Despicable, don't ever do that."

When Raymond found out that Silvia's previous relationship had ended, he acted quickly. He asked her out within days of the event. This approach took a little getting used to for Silvia. It all turned out fine though. Not only the children but Raymond's cats were no problem at all.

"I sat there at home on the couch, enjoying my aunt Greet's birthday party. Out of the blue my sister phoned and said: 'Hey, Silvia, come over here for a while, you have a secret admirer.' That was the day that Rob, my brother in law had bumped into Raymond. He had asked Rob how I was doing and when he found out I was on my own again, wanted to know if I would be at all interested in going out on a date. 'Who's Raymond van Barneveld?' I asked my sister, quizzically. I couldn't remember meeting him in Zandvoort at all.

That Monday he was supposed to come into The Concurrant. I knew that the family had arranged for Raymond to come over and I was extremely nervous about it. In the back of my mind I knew that my mother thought I would never be totally happy without a man in my life.

The first question Raymond asked me that evening was: 'Do you go out on dates nowadays?' I mumbled some kind of reply like: 'Not if I don't like the look of him, I don't.' After that one-liner statement, Raymond didn't come near me again for weeks! It was a coincidence when we did meet again. A few weeks later, there he was, walking into the bar. Normally I wouldn't have been working that evening but my uncle had been taken ill, strange? This time he managed to build up the courage to speak to me for a while. In fact we went as red as beetroots when we saw each other again. The signs were apparent for all to see, we were already in love. Mind you it was only towards the end of the evening, that he mentioned he really liked me a lot. 'But, I am not a single girl any more. I have two children', I said. '...And I have three cats', replied Raymond."

The first date was on the 19th December 1992. There they were, an extremely shy Raymond meeting the equally nervous Silvia. She still remembers it well: "Yes, it was our first date, important, so the question was, what should I wear? I chose a green top coupled with a black skirt. One advantage was that my parents already knew him. I lived with my grandparents at the time, next door to my parents and we started the evening off there. It was true that Raymond had to shake a lot of hands before we were allowed to go off to see the film but he already knew some of my relations. I was taught this courtesy a long time back. Before you start going out with someone, first introduce them to everyone. None of that 'Hello, goodbye we're off', stuff that happens a lot nowadays. We went to the Cineac, a cinema in the centre of The Hague, which is called Pathé Buitenhof these days. We saw Home Alone 2. I laughed myself silly, more at Raymond than at the film. He was creased-up in the seat, laughing. During the movie we stole our first kiss on his up-take. I may have a big mouth but I'm quite shy really. After that we drove out of The Hague to The Hook of Holland and sat there in his green Ford Escort. Watching the ships. Very romantic!"

Raymond kissing his wife Silvia just before his sensational victory at the PDC WK in 2007.

The first two weeks were great but then darts commitments caused a problem between them for the first time. "Just when we were starting to get to know each other better, he had to go off to England for the 1993 Embassy. We both suffered the pangs of love. We phoned each other every day and both of us would have loved it, if he could have come straight back home. People have since asked me how I fell in love with Raymond so quickly. It was because of the attention, love and care that he gave me. He wanted to make me feel comfortable. I just knew he was the one for me, plain and simple. I felt comfortable around him. I loved the look in his eyes. When you first meet someone and fall in love, everything is magic. This translates into wanting to be with someone all the time. You love each other more and more each day. Even up to this day. Every day. At the beginning of our relationship it was really difficult for me to adjust. I had just come out of an episode where I had been in love with someone else. Now I had fallen in love again, this time with Raymond. I really hoped that it would turn into the real thing but I was also scared that it might not. Luckily it all went well. Especially from the moment we picked him up from the boat at the Hoek of Holland, the relationship really took off then. We went straight home and picked up some things from his place. He moved straight in with me and has never left again! Back then I was still living in my parent's attic room on the Maasstraat. I had just been given benefits and the key to a new rental home from a housing association. As I didn't want to make any big decisions in a hurry, I cancelled the option on the house. Raymond understood and supported me, as he did with most things at the time. He went through a lot, standing by me through my ongoing grief. Luckily my parents gave us the space that our relationship needed. It all came together well. My parents were actually raising my children during that time.

Right from the offset Raymond was kind and very patient with the children. One day he took Mike to McDonald's and they had a great day together. However when they got home, with no forewarning, Mike went and gave Raymond a slap on the face, saying: 'You're not my father.' Raymond went straight down on his knees to be on his level and said kindly: 'I know that I'm not your father, Mike, but I'm still your very best friend... and I love you.' Now then! The tears were rolling down my cheeks. Wow, what a sensitive man. I was not expecting that, it was the first time I had seen this all-caring side of Raymond. Right from the start he was great with Daisy too. Giving her a bottle and changing her nappies in his own sweet way. Ha, Ha, of course that was not the smoothest running task to undertake for him as a man but he got through it. Not very well, but he did get through it! Now everything started moving very fast. One minute Raymond was single and had no responsibilities and the next, all of a sudden he was a father to two kids. Then…Along came a third, which was actually not the plan. Hmm, if only the doctor had prescribed a stronger contraception pill? Raymond was in effect suddenly thrown to the lions. Mind you, not once did he make a problem of that and nor did his parents. He was deeply in love and wanted to give it all a chance. Sometimes I could see in his behaviour, that he didn't always know how to handle it all. I also realise I had a very inquisitive family, so quite a few of them kept their eye on him. It turned out that he passed that test with flying colours."

The first place that they moved into together was on the Ijsselstraat, number 22. Their daughter Patty was also born there. "When I fell pregnant we still lived with my parents. Our new house needed decorating from top to bottom. Fortunately the entire family was willing to help us with it. Raymond I'm afraid, wasn't up to much at all. He could hardly hang a painting. I was around five months pregnant when we moved. Patty was born on 11th February 1994. Raymond first heard the news from my grandmother that he was to be a father. He came home on his post office bicycle as usual and before he had even stepped into the house, he was told the news. It all started to seem a bit scary now. How were we going to manage?"

The three children Daisy, Patty and Mike cheering Raymond on during the World Darts Trophy held in 2003.

Thanks to the assistance of the Social, an interest free loan and a healthy appetite for work, the young couple managed to make it through their first couple of years together. Although they didn't have much money at all: "During the first few years of our relationship it was a daily struggle to stay financially afloat. But usually by the time things started to look pretty bad, Raymond would manage to win a tournament somewhere and we would be okay again for a while. But then maybe the car would break down again or the washing machine would go u/s. You name it, if it happened, and it would, we had no money left again. If by any chance we didn't have a problem in any one month, we would use the excess to pay the rent in advance, just in case. We kept sticking all the bills on the fridge. 'This month pay this but not that etc., etc'. If we fell behind on some rental payments it would mean, that until he had won something else we were struggling to pay the debts. Raymond had to do this juggling all the time, at the outset. He hated debt and always wanted everything paid in full, on time if possible. Unfortunately we had periods when it just wouldn't work out. 'How in heavens name are we going to make it through the week?' we used to think sometimes. A nice day trip with the kids to an amusement park like the Efteling hadn't been made in years. Counting our blessings, we did always manage to have food on the table each day. Raymond spent everything he made on his family. I remember one hot summer evening he came home, after having won a tournament, with 2 big boxes full of ice cream. He handed it out to all the children playing at the time in the local playground."

The relationship grew stronger and slowly Silvia got to know the real Raymond: "He still kept himself very much to himself in the beginning. Raymond used to stay at home most of the time. He didn't like sitting in the sun or any sort of hustle or bustle around him. If I asked him to come and sit with me for a while, he would do that, maybe for half an hour or so. Then he would go upstairs again and do something on his PC. Actually he has always been a bit of a loner. Definitely no big party animal. I do know though that he used to play lots of games with his parents when he lived at home. My family are wind-up merchants, they like to cheat at games. He couldn't stand that. Games had to be played fairly and if they weren't it would upset him a lot."

Raymond and Silvia: Still inseparable.

Raymond made Silvia's dream come true, when he asked her to marry him.

Losing the final but winning the girl

The relationship was a strong one. Raymond, more romantic than people thought, decided in 1995 to make Silvia's dream come true and marry her, after his breakthrough at The Embassy.

Raymond: "You never know at the beginning, if someone really is the right one for you. It's only when, slowly but surely you get to know one another better, that the whole picture unfolds. I gradually discovered that Silvia was as true, honest and sweet as I thought she was from the beginning. She really wanted to get married as well. When I reached *The Embassy* final in 1995 I won quite a bit of money. At the same time my dream had come true. Even though I had lost in the final, I was very happy I had managed to reach the runner-up position. I had always wanted to see: Dutch darts in the charts!

Even though had I lost in the final, I still asked Silvia to marry me. I wanted to make her dream come true as well. I proposed to her as we were lying in bed, soon after. We just hugged each other and she said yes.

Actually the whole marriage, wedding thing started with my mother in law. A while before we were walking in town and I suggested that we buy friendship rings. Just because... I came home and the first thing my mother-in-law said was: 'Wonderful, Saturday there's going to be a party, okay. All you need to do is hand over Dfl 500 and I'll organise you both an engagement party.' I don't think there are very many people out there like my in-laws. There're great and always ready to help. My parents are less like that and it bothers me sometimes. Silvia's parents give help to whoever needs it, including us. They may come over and cook a meal for example, or help out generally. I can't remember ever having had a cross word with them since the day we met.

One day I was watching a programme on television about millionaires. Specifically people who had won the jackpot and could afford anything they wished for. A new car, home, you name it. Silvia said casually to me that I was exactly the person who could give our family this type of wealth and bright future. Right there and then I decided I would and could make a go of it, as she said. Guess what, she was right! I started focusing and realised that I had my destiny in my own hands. Everyone had always mentioned to me that they thought I was a talented darts player. So now I had a family setting motivating me, I wanted to prove them all correct. The timing was perfect. I felt good, comfortable and relaxed about life. I would also go out for a run sometimes. I had a good job with the postal services, earned a decent wage and was home every day at around one in the afternoon. Which still left me lots of time to do other things. Not to mention that good money was stating to come in, competing in tournaments as well. This was more of a necessary income source than a hobby though, as there were always bills to be paid. I might win Dfl 750 at a tournament on a Sunday but by the following Friday my car exhaust pipe might have fallen off. Crash! Dfl 900 out the coffers, just like that. Back to square one again!

In 1994, the year that the PDC split from the BDO, all of a sudden there were two darts organisations. At the time I was sponsored by Harrows. Martin van der Linden of HD Sports, who represented Harrows in The Netherlands, wanted me to join the PDC. At that point I didn't want to myself. I was being cautious. It felt too early, as I had only just started my international career. I realised that because of his sponsoring concerns he tried to push things along a little, as they wanted a Dutchman linked to the PDC.

In 1995 Raymond married Silvia. The wedding was partly paid for with Raymond's winnings from being runner-up in The Embassy final, the same year.

The PDC had a difficult initiation period. Phil Taylor told me once, that he didn't win prize money in the beginning but shares. He still has these and quite a few at that. I wasn't very happy with this possible outcome. It would mean that, I wouldn't be able to play for my country any longer but also not in the Dutch LACO. I would also be barred from playing in The Hague leagues, or any other competitions and tournaments that I played in regularly. There were big play-off considerations to bear in mind, if you changed over at that time. These were not compensated with the lure of major prize money, as is now the case. Yes, the founder members of the PDC had a very difficult time, all in all. With hindsight I think that, when the PDC was established in 1994, it opened up a great opportunity at the BDO for me. Around twenty of the best darters in the world left the BDO in an instant. That made a big difference! All the other names like Baxter, Burnett and Adams, were unknown entities to me, so they carried no awe in my eyes. Very quickly however I discovered that these guys were awesome dart-players.

The '95 Embassy was a major career highlight. I was placed again because of my position in the international rankings. I managed to start out pretty well in the tournament. I opened against the Scott Les Wallace, throwing 180 nine times in first round! I won narrowly 3-2. He was a challenge but I had never even heard of him before. In the ensuing years that would all change though. After that I won the second round 3-0, beating Dave Askew. In the quarterfinal playing against Colin Monk I won 4-2 and then via a tight 5-4 sets victory against Martin Adams, I managed to reach the final. That was one unforgettable and special winning streak, during a great tournament.

I had agreed beforehand with Roland 'Tripod' Scholten, that we would share any prize money 50/50, whatever. Back then that was par for the course. As he was disqualified in the first round against Monk, our agreement worked out very well for him. If I'm honest, just reaching the final was a good enough reward for me. Satisfaction can take you in two directions. You may end up being so happy that you get complacent and you don't play that well, or you feel so great that you end up throwing twice as good as usual. My opponent in the final, Richie Burnett was obviously a wonderful darts player but I missed far too many doubles during the game.

Dutch TV's *Studio Sport* transmitted the game live. That was great for my image at home. It was a pity I lost in the end but sometimes when I reflect on it, I still feel, deep down that I was glad at the time that I ended as runner up and not the winner. After all, the number two didn't have to make a speech at the closing banquet, I thought. The evening before the final I broke into a sweat, thinking about having to do just that. My God, I was not looking forward to it at all and I meant it from the bottom of my heart. What I didn't know then was that the runner-up also had to make a speech!"

Having to address an audience has always been Raymond's worst nightmare. Here, acting as the ADO The Hague football club ambassador, he thanks all The ADO fans on the terraces for their support.

Reaching the final of *The Embassy* brought about a turning point for **Silvia** and for their relationship. Silvia had to handle and adjust to his fame very quickly. "Raymond started winning round after round there. Then suddenly, there in front of him was a sponsorship deal, worth in the region of Dfl 5.000. That was it! He discussed it all with his friend Fred Vrolijk, a great man who worked in the building industry for a local construction company in The Hague. Fred came back to The Netherlands, called on me and said: 'I have come to fetch you, we are going to England.' I didn't have any money spare for this little event, of course. Fred said, no worries, he would pay for the trip. I really didn't know what I had got myself into during my first visit to Frimley Green. I didn't speak a word of English. 'What in God's name are you going to do here', I thought. It was a big surprise for Raymond when I arrived. The other players were not happy at all, seeing Raymond go the distance. Yet another non-Englishman on the scene, who, just as John Part did in 1994, was now capable of winning the trophy.

I'm afraid to say but I thought the food being served up there was disgusting. Hamburger and fries, nothing special at all. I didn't know anyone either. To crown it all it seemed a very stately affair. Imagine, all these old men in their red jackets prancing around. I thought these old boys were security, but it turned out they were big wig officials from the BDO."

Still, the food, the cold shoulder and even the language barrier were not to be the worst things Silvia had to endure at the Lakeside Country Club that year. The BBC's camera's that were to be focused on her turned out to be much more of an ordeal: "When I heard I would soon be on camera I was terrified. I felt awful. I was quite big at the time and I hadn't expected to be on UK TV. There I was, with a double chin, wearing a simple T-shirt and no money to go to the hairdresser. After Raymond had won the semi-final I ended up in the VIP area. In the same area was also a pressroom, with a long row of telephones. The manager of the pressroom, Robert Holmes, was walking around there and I also noticed someone typing. The phones seemed to be constantly ringing. It was the Dutch press phoning for the latest news about Raymond and before I knew it, I was answering calls from here there and everywhere. They all kept phoning in. The nicest thing was when I received a call on one of the lines from my parents and father in law. The whole episode was becoming unreal though. It was frantic and even the Dutch TV phoned. I didn't know what to do or say at all. In the end it was just Raymond, Fred and I there on our own. Then Mart Smeets, a famous Dutch TV presenter called and wanted us on his Dutch sports programme. Would we go to the studio as soon as we got back to The Netherlands? A representative from the town hall of The Hague also phoned in. 'How did Raymond wish to be welcomed home?' and… 'How many people could come over to the final in the UK?' and 'How should that be arranged?' 'Okay, okay, okay. Well, I didn't know did I?' I had just arrived myself, having been taken out and away from my sitting room in a frenzy of activity, just the day before."

Silvia was completely out of her depth, she realised afterwards. "Everything went so fast there, it was very strange, surreal. okay, Raymond lost the final but I still experienced everything as a big high. 'With hindsight I was much too trusting', she now says. When I arrived home I found a long interview with me had been printed in a Dutch magazine. I then remembered the conversation I had with a woman at the bar where the event was taking place in England. I remember thinking at the time that everyone seemed very nice and meant well. I told her my whole life story, including the breakup with Marcel and so on. Everything was in there. Everything that was written was true, so it could not be denied but I had obviously not meant for it to be publicised. At that point, there in England, I was very vulnerable. I wanted to talk to someone and I thought I could trust this woman. She only wanted to ask me a few questions. The thought I was used upset me very much."

The effect on her life became even more apparent after they had arrived home. As if they had walked back into a different world: "The '95 Embassy trip turned into an enormous lesson for me. It was unbelievable. I arrived home and the mayor of The Hague, Burgemeester Havermans was waiting for us in our living room! My aunt was there answering the phone, and there were loads of postbags full of mail laying around. Everyone was opening letters, from all over the country. The most impressive gift was a bouquet of flowers from Dutch judo champion Anton Geesink. My Father had been a judoka and he admired this man enormously. The bouquet of flowers was a welcome surprise amid all the hustle and bustle. We didn't have a lot of time to fully appreciate what was going on though. We had to get changed and rush out again immediately, as Raymond had to be at the TV studio. I walked around in my jeans, sports shoes and a lumberjack shirt. 'Oh,' Smeets retorted, after he found out that I was with Raymond, 'I thought you were part of the editorial staff.' Yes well, we didn't have any money spare for nice clothes in those days. What followed was pretty hectic. There hadn't been time to let anything sink in properly. There came along, in short order, interviews, television and so on. Samsonite also phoned to say that they wanted to present us with a suitcase set. That never happened in the end and there were many other things like that. Why do all these people suddenly phone you?"

With the prize money Raymond had won at *The Embassy* he paid off all the outstanding bills. What was left over, Silvia was able to use to finance their wedding. "To be able to be married in a 'Sissi' dress was always my greatest dream. The only thing missing on my parent's wall was a wedding photo of me and my bridegroom. My brother and sister's were already up there. There was just one empty space left."

It was on 20th October 1995 that Raymond van Barneveld and Silvia began married life, a Friday. They were married in the Blue Room at the Old City Town Hall on the Dagelijkse Groenmarkt in The Hague. It was a great day: "I had ordered a limousine for us. When it arrived everyone was already waiting outside in the road. Later, we drove around The Hague for the entire day in a double-decker bus with eighty people on board. In the evening we had organised a party for 260 people in the Postkoets. It was an expensive wedding. In the end, it cost around Dfl 25.000 but that was okay. During the day, when we were sitting down having a rest, we opened the envelopes that were given to us as presents, to count the money. There were also empty envelopes. Some even without a card inside. Unbelievable! If you don't have any money to spare, at least give us a card but no, hey. Even on such a nice day you still have to face things like that. Obviously there was someone out there who really didn't like us that much. That hurt a lot."

The wedding turned out to be the start of a busy but less happy period. Even though the real lows would only show themselves later. "Raymond desperately wanted to turn professional, but continued playing darts only part time, for another few years. A fortune-teller told Raymond once, that he would end up always being the eternal runner-up. He couldn't let go of that, so he would withdraw even more than usual into his room, watching movies and playing music. 'Everything will be fine in the end', I always told him. Life was tense sometimes. For instance, when Raymond was interviewed at home, the kids and I would have to sit in the kitchen, like dumbo's. Playing a game with dolls, cars or whatever, until he was finished. He really had to concentrate during an interview. If he got distracted he would get irritated with us and things could go wrong."

A magical, triumphant moment, being shared by Raymond with Ad Schoofs, his manager.

Highs, lows and Ad Schoofs

Reaching the 1995 Embassy final that year was the absolute highlight of Raymond van Barneveld's career to date. Despite losing, reaching the final of the most prestigious darts tournament in the world made him believe, that everything was now possible to achieve in the darts world. The following years however, like so many times before in his life, were characterised by a series of personal disappointments.

"After the '95 final the first bookings started rolling in for demo darting events. I really hoped to be able to find sponsors to support my dart playing, leading to a better quality of life. I had always dreamed of becoming a professional and wanted to leave the PTT. Not because of any problems at work but because I wanted to become a professional player ASAP. For a full two years I hoped it would happen. Right up until '97, when I eventually said to myself: 'Hey, it's not going to happen, forget it.' I reasoned that I should adjust my mind to enjoying the game again and shouldn't dream of unachievable goals any more. So once again darts became just an enjoyable pastime, drawing in a moderate extra income, and nothing more.

Everyone who had wanted to sponsor me earlier moved back into the shadows. At one stage many 'vultures' had tried to come down and peck out a living on my earlier success. In the end I had to make a selection from ten agencies. For me it was important that they could make demonstration events happen and provide a good sponsor. Everyone promised a lot but nobody came up with anything concrete. Eventually a company named Topsport Marketing, NR.10, owned by Maarten de Vos, came in for me. They then started to handle all my business matters. By then I had already done a lot of demonstration events including Hans Verkerk Kitchens, a big name in The Netherlands. As a result of these types of shows, a demo circuit unfolded. This also of course in turn helped to stimulate my income. I remember the time well. Once I had a booking in Breda scheduled for the Friday, one in Belgium on the Saturday and one following in Zeeland in the south west of The Netherlands, on the Sunday. Roland Scholten and I drove home on the Sunday evening laughing. I had Dfl 3.500 tucked away safely in my pocket. All of a sudden though, as we were driving past the Princeville restaurant in Breda the car engine blew-up. We had to call out the ANWB, a Dutch version of the AA. They picked us up and dropped us off home safely. The cost of the repair: Dfl 3.800. It made me feel sick. But yes, when we totalled up all the income from my other bookings, we had still managed to scrape up enough money to go on holiday. Our first vacation was to the Center Parcs holiday resort, De Eemhof in Flevoland, located about an hours' drive from the centre of Amsterdam. It was wonderful, a week away with my family and in-laws. It was a shame that a longer holiday wasn't possible but it was good while it lasted. For the first time in my life I felt I was getting somewhere. Being able to qualify for *The Embassy* each year was earning me quite a bit, even based on the start money of Dfl 6.000, each time. This amount I put aside for a rainy day. It was a lot of money for our family to receive, in those days."

The hopeless ongoing search for a sponsor made performing on the night a must. Up until halfway through the 90's the world of darts had still only heard of one real darts tournament: *The Embassy*. So it was extremely important for Raymond to perform there to the best of his ability. Once upon a time Frimley Green was the holy grail of his darts-hobby. Now though, this darts competition, held yearly within a large village setting in Surrey, was more of a UK darts stronghold that Raymond simply had to conquer. Only there, could he draw maximum attention.

Raymond's first international triumph of note was achieved by winning the Grand Masters of 1995, held in the Grote Kerk, The Hague. The Englishman Martin Adams was his opponent on that day and turned out to be Raymond's opponent in several other finals down the years. (Photo: Jos van Leeuwen.)

"In both '96 and '97 I was knocked out of *The Embassy* in the second round. In '96, against the Englishman, Matt Clark and in '97 against the Scot, Les Wallace. Both years I won in the first round 3-0. The first time against the Belgian Leo Laurens and a year later against the Welshman Sean Palfrey. Not very good performances at all. I still kept persevering but never managed to match my dream target as a semi-pro. It was only when I was able to let go of my dream to become a full professional that my best years followed. With, as the reward, capturing the 1998 Embassy title. After beating the Englishman Michael Marshall 3 sets to 1 in the first round of this tournament, I began by trailing 2-0 against Andy Fordham in the second. The 2nd round seemed to be developing into a mental hurdle for me. However I managed to overcome my block and went on from there to win 9 of the next 10 legs. That was bizarre. Both the third and fourth sets I won 3 legs to 0 and the last I came out 3-1 up. Not only had I beaten Andy 3 sets to 2, I had also reached the quarterfinals. I'm quite sure I was given some intervention from above in 1998. Andy didn't manage to throw many decent darts in the game, whilst I had a great match.

Again, in the quarterfinal against Steve Beaton, everything went smoothly. On the day Steve seemed helpless to pull the stops out against me. Fortunately I had now managed to delete this mental barrier to winning the second round and won 5-0. It proved a lot harder to reach the semi-final against Steve's fellow countryman Colin Monk though. Colin was in tip-top form that year and gave me a hard time. Before our game I started mulling over the possibility of reaching a second Embassy final. 'Wouldn't it be great to reach it a second time and even maybe…' No, I didn't dare think further at that point, I had more pressing issues to think about. I had to beat Monk first…and I did in the end. As the game closed, there, in lights, stood a convincing 5-3 on the scoreboard. Yes, I was able to move on to experience my dream. Competing in my second Embassy final.

Guess what? It turned out that of all people, Richie Burnett, the man who had beaten me in the 1995 final, was to be my opponent, once again. It was a game full of tension and drama as you might expect. I began by winning two sets in a row: the first 3-1 and then a 3-2 leg win. Next Burnett won two sets, 3-0 and 3-1. We followed on by each winning another 2 sets by the same leg margin, 3-2 and then I won my 5th set 3 legs to 0. He went on to draw level 5 sets all, with a 3 leg to 1, set win. The score now 5-5. The eleventh set was to be the deciding one. As the advantage in this set went backwards and forwards, we counter balanced each other constantly, up until we had reached 2 legs all. Then I managed to creep ahead by winning the next leg, taking the score to 3-2, before also triumphantly winning the following 4th and deciding leg, a requirement for the final play-off. I had finally secured my first ever Embassy title!

Up to this point all I had experienced in the darts world was a lot of teasing and Mickey taking. Only light heartedly of course. If I did something that they thought I could improve on, in would go the one-liner. The boys would tell me, straight in my face, to encourage me, keep on my toes and improve. Right up 'til that day, that was, the 11th January 1998, when I closed out from 76 and went down on my knees in a state of euphoria. At that moment, all at once, eleven long years of pent-up emotions came to the surface. Everything that I had been through, up to that point, came out. The unhappiness, all the frustrations and my never-ending lack of self-esteem, came flooding into my mind and I was in tears. The sheer knowing that you are now a world champion, so proving to everyone that you could do it, overwhelmed me.

After the final was won I still had one more difficult job to complete. Remember? As a finalist, I had to make a speech at the tournament dinner. Luckily I had already taken this possibility into account. I had prepared two speeches. One for if I lost and another for if I won. Unfortunately the press assumed that I had only prepared a winning speech and labelled me as over confident. But that's my style; I try to prepare as much as possible before an event. I was very nervous at the time though. I'm naturally very shy, so having to stand up and address hundreds of people, was an epic task for me. Not to mention having to make the speech in English! I willed myself to be calm at the time, which seemed to help and thought to myself that people would understand, even if my English wasn't perfect.

Raymond celebrating his first win at The Embassy in 1998. Unbelievable! A Dutchman makes off with The Embassy title! An almost impossible achievement to imagine at the time. Raymond won through after beating Richie Burnett in a tense final. (Photo: Steve Daszko.)

Eventually everything worked out fine on the night and I went to sleep feeling great."

Raymond on bended knees, just after he had thrown the final winning dart at The Embassy in 1998. (Photo: Steve Daszko.)

Also, instantly The Netherlands was able to see and cheer their new darting phenomenon: Raymond van Barneveld. Because of Dutch TV and media attention around 1, 3 million people had been able to watch the final on SBS6 that day and probably at least as many had followed the final via the BBC cable broadcast. Everywhere things were buzzing. The entire population of The Netherlands seemed to be talking about the friendly postman from The Hague, who had done something really amazing while playing darts in England. Obviously the high level of attention was also due to the fact that there's a lack of other sporting events held in early January.Apart from darts, there was only ski jumping or alternatively a skating tournament being broadcast. These two events did not provide much competition, or overshadow the

formidable achievement that Raymond made. All of a sudden a sort of Barney-mania sprung up. The NDF, the Dutch Darts Federation now re-named the NDB, the Nederlandse Darts Bond, organised the Dutch Darts League. They noted quickly, that the popularity of their sport was growing. Dartboards and arrows were selling fast. In fact what Raymond had actually done on the 11th of January was not only win a tournament. He had, this being at least equally important, stimulated the creation of a breeding ground, in The Netherlands, for future talent. From the new generation of young Dutchmen who made their breakthrough in the darts world since 2005, there have been quite a few who were first inspired by Raymond's successes, starting with his first Embassy-win in 1998.

Something else also changed in Raymond's life. He was meeting people who could and would be able to help him get ahead. People who could open up career opportunities for him. It was shortly after his first Embassy success that Raymond met Ad Schoofs. He originated from Brabant in the south of The Netherlands and worked for the Chiel van Praag, InterShow. Schoofs arranged bookings for artists. The difference between Schoofs and others in the business was, that he realised very early on, that there wasn't much difference between booking an artist or a top dart player. This awareness led to a long-term, close and special relationship between the two being formed.

"Ad revealed to me later that he had been watching the 1998 Embassy with his daughter at home when, right there and then, he had an idea. It was of arranging a promotional touring car to travel up and down the Dutch coast, with the aim of introducing people into the world of darts. Additionally, he asked me if I would consider hosting openings. This particular idea I liked. At that time Ron van Noort was already my manager and he was good. Ron then organised one or two sponsors for me. We had also formed a Dutch VOF at the chamber of commerce, a legally recognised partnership. Unfortunately this was one of my big mistakes. It turned out that Ron was not effective enough with his negotiations to bring larger sponsors to the table. When I decided to move on though, I had to pay him off as a partner, rather than as a manager.

Ad had no idea how to get hold of me. With the assistance of The Hague police he found out where I normally played darts. That's where we first met. Ron was there too. Right from the off set Ad and I clicked, even though he had no intention to become my manager. He only wanted to get me demo dart bookings. At the time I had people contacting me left, right and centre but after meeting Ad I immediately felt comfortable. The deciding factor for me was the fact that Ad worked for Chiel van Praag, InterShow. A well-known and respected outfit that produced some popular Dutch TV shows. Chiel also presented some of these shows and I liked him straight away.

A few days after we arranged to work together, I asked Ad to come with us to a Dutch insurance company. They had invited Ron and myself over, to talk about a possible sponsorship deal. With hindsight, Ad's presence at this meeting turned out to be very important. Not so much because of the sponsorship angle but because Ron made some unprofessional remarks. At the time we were talking about a main sponsorship agreement and that would entail lots of money. In the midst of the negotiations Ron suddenly piped up and said: 'If the deal goes ahead, I suppose I will be eligible to sign up for a cheap mortgage with you.' Just like that, in the middle of the discussions. I immediately looked up and saw Ad eye Ron as if he was from another planet. This was not the reason why the deal fell through in the end but I'm sure it didn't help much either!

Yvonne Paling from the insurance company, a very pleasant lady, was also very enthusiastic. She said that she would explain the whole strategy to her management and was sure that everyone would vote for it. The insurer was even going to discuss the possibility of pumping money into Dutch darts, via the NDF. The whole plan sounded great, but was not finalised in the end. One person in management, high up in the company, did not take to the idea, so in the end it didn't happen. I remember saying to Ad at this point that it was probably blocked by someone who wouldn't be working there in three months time. Believe it or not but that's exactly what happened.

When we walked out into the insurance company's car park after the meeting, Ad encouraged me to think carefully about having Ron as my manager. I replied, that I would take his advice but asked if he would be available as my manager instead. He didn't expect this but there was nobody else I knew that could do the job. Ad acted sensibly concerning the offer, wanting to think about it first. He phoned me a little while later and said he would accept my offer. But then I had another problem, how to say goodbye to Ron first. That business partnership goodbye cost me Dfl 10,000. In fact everything I had managed to earn up to that point. I was in a way 'grateful' to him for accepting this payoff. The reason being, I either had to pay off Ron at the time, or I would have had to give him half of what I was offered, should I receive a good sponsorship deal. This would have been because of our business agreement. Ad had foreseen this possibility and forewarned me. So I decided to buy out of the partnership I had with Ron.

Before we even officially started our adventure together we had a fun moment. Along with Ad I walked into the Fortis Bank in The Hague, to deposit the cheque I'd received for winning *The Embassy*. We were welcomed by Ronald Mallée, who was the branch manager at the time and is still to this day my advisor. Just as we were walking to Ronald's office, Ad answered his phone. I asked him to cut the call short as we were going in there. Ad shushed me frantically: 'Keep quiet, the insurance company is on the line and in the market to fund an enormous amount of money per year!' Obviously, knowing this, I didn't care any more how long he was going to be on the phone for..."

When describing Ad Schoofs, the word manager is a bit of an understatement. He also became Raymond's personal secretary, driver, coach, friend and much more. A special emotional bond developed between the two of them.

Ad Schoofs didn't have any special contact with the darts world before he had a glimpse of Raymond performing live on the television that day. It only started seizing his imagination when he got caught up in the drama of it. "When I watched *The Embassy* final on that Sunday, 11th January 1998, my excitement built with his every throw. I imagine it was the same for every Dutchman who was watching. Even at this stage there were a few ideas racing through my mind. In an interview Raymond stated he definitely wanted to become a professional darts player, that he had been looking for a sponsor for a long time but none had come forward yet. The following Tuesday I went to an exhibition, where I met a dealer for electronic soft tip darts cases. Our discussions led on to Raymond and his achievements. I went back that evening but before going home went into the office, to think what I might be able to do for a world champion dart player.

At that time I worked at the artist and event bookings office of Chiel van Praag InterShow and saw in Raymond an artist, of sorts. He had already managed to establish himself with a high public profile, so he could do openings and bookings. I saw the idea of promoting Raymond as a company project and didn't think for one minute that there could be a manager's role in the offering. On the Wednesday morning, after the final, I started phoning round immediately, to try and locate him. In the end I phoned the police in The Hague, because the only details I had were, his name, Van Barneveld and the fact that he lived in The Hague. It didn't look like it would be nearly enough information to trace him. The police kindly referred me to the Carrousel Bar, where I managed to speak to the owner, Cor Tuurenhout. Back then the Carrousel was Raymond's local. Cor put me in touch with Raymond's manager, Ron van Noort.

A short telephone conversation with Ron followed, in which I relayed my intentions to him and told him also that I also had some potential candidates, who could be interested in a sponsorship deal. This info prompted them to invite me for a meeting at 11:00am on Saturday, 17th January at the IJsselstraat 22. We tuned into the same business wavelength, pretty quickly. There was an immediate feeling of mutual trust. Maybe it was partly because I didn't turn up wearing a suit and tie, like others had before but smart casual. Two hours chatting, that's all it took.

A week later Raymond phoned. He wanted me to accompany him to an insurance company. Initially the meeting went very well. They wanted to sponsor Raymond, to the tune of a large sum of money. Additionally, they wanted to throw in a few hundred thousand guilders for training. So there was a lot of money involved. I wasn't Raymond's manager, so I just sat there as an observer.

On the way out, once I had time to digest the way that the meeting had proceeded, I knew it hadn't gone well. It seemed to be the result of a couple of remarks that Ron had made. At that juncture I thanked Raymond for his interest in me, in InterShow and inviting me along that day. I must be honest though, I wasn't really looking forward to working with Ron, after this eye opener. Raymond said he wanted to think it all over. So I put the event to the back of my mind. The very next day though Raymond phoned and asked straight out if I would become his manager. Events then started to move extremely fast. Chiel was away on a winter sports holiday. I phoned to tell him that I had the green light to represent Raymond van Barneveld, for making his bookings and so on. Chiel seemed somewhat cautious on hearing the news. The same evening however, at the hotel where Chiel was staying, the only topic of conversation was Van Barneveld …and then the penny suddenly dropped. He knew it would be the right thing to do. Deep into the night, there I was, listening to a phone call from him, asking if I had signed him yet.

"A few weeks after my partnership with Ron was dissolved, a new candidate for main sponsorship came in for me. Brandstaff, the Dutch employment agency. They had congratulated me on my Embassy triumph, by placing a full-page ad in the *De Telegraaf*. Ron was very upset at the time, that they used my name for publicity, without even asking us. Ad however had a very different take on this and phoned them soon after he became my manager. That move eventually resulted in an attractive sponsorship contract and later led to the Brandstaff Masters tournament being initiated. This was in 1999, the first, big, open invitation tournament to be held in The Netherlands. It was fantastic. All the top players in the world played there."

Schoofs was tied in very closely with the deal involving Brandstaff: "Actually, I had realised straight away, that the deal with the Insurance Company would not go through. It started me thinking though. So that same week I sat round the table with the Brandstaff guys. I just phoned their head office in Eindhoven. I spoke to Jenneke Sonneveld. She was Brandstaff's managing director and we made an appointment to meet the following Friday. During our conversation I told her I needed an answer before 12:00 midday the following Monday. This was because there were some other interested parties but I would prefer to be associated with Brandstaff. One reason being, that Barney and Brandstaff both began with a 'B', which could be used as a sales gimmick. This was pure sales talk, I might add. That Monday morning at 10:00 am Jenneke phoned me to ask if I would drive down to Eindhoven and sign a letter of intent. The amount: Dfl 350.000 per year, for a total of three years. One million and fifty thousand Dutch guilders in total! Wow! At this time a figure as large as this was unheard of for sponsoring a dart player. Even in England nobody earned that much!

I was a total stranger to the world of darts and had absolutely no idea who was important and why. At this point in his career, Raymond was very impressed with the people at the BDO. He was also in great awe of the big names. For example, in the final of the Brandstaff Masters, Raymond had to play against Martin Adams. He was quite apprehensive about this duel. I just knew. On top of this, he put himself under enormous pressure, because he desperately wanted to win the tournament. Then I used a trick that had worked for me in the past, in a different situation. I just walked up to Raymond and told him I had heard Martin Adams mention to a few supporters, that he would annihilate him and that the Dutchman had no chance of winning the tournament, backed by his own sponsor. Even more, I told him Adams had said that he would humiliate him. This was all done with some personal knowledge of how Raymond's mind worked. Guess what, just as I expected, Raymond was furious. I even saw the 'Eye of the Tiger'-look in his eyes for the first time. It came as no surprise that he beat Adams that day."

This was a tournament Raymond really had to win: the first Brandstaff Masters and he did. Note the worried expression on the face of Martin Fitzmaurice (l), who looks visibly unhappy with the Dutch hero's win.

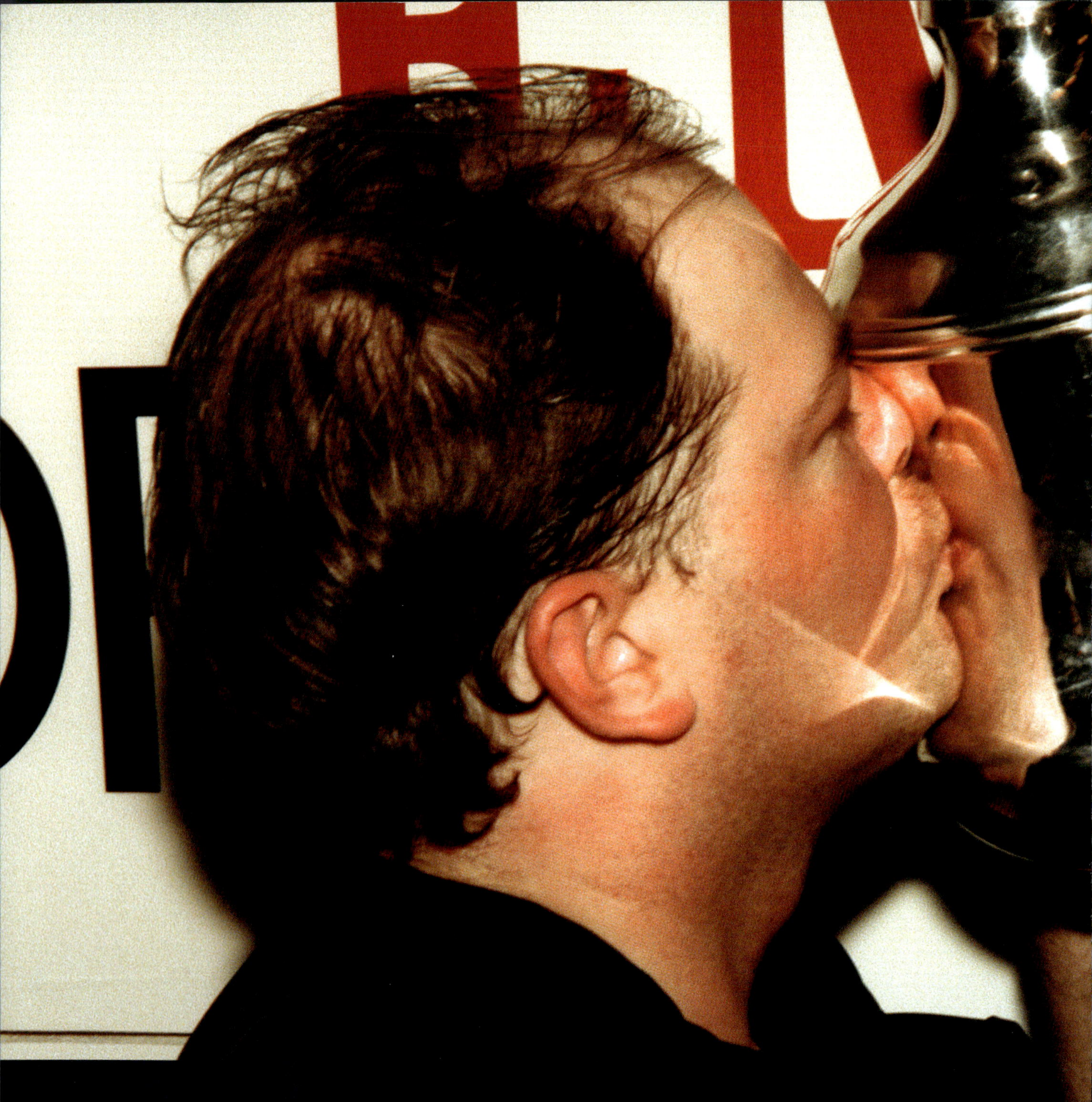

Barney kissing the trophy that meant so much to him, also in 1999.

Everlasting fame

After his fantastic win at The Embassy in 1998, Raymond knew that all eyes would be on him the following year. He felt the pressure of having to achieve. Achieve in the name of the sport, his country and naturally, for himself. He in effect, put this pressure on himself and was driven to defend his title. Also, the darts-hype that was slowly sweeping through The Netherlands could not be allowed to fade away. A loss in the first, or the dreaded second round was unimaginable.

Raymond's emergence as a top dart player was a major discussion topic that year. Before the match he stepped onto the stage with the "Return of the Legend" yellow and green scarf that ADO Den Haag football fans had designed especially to commemorate their cup game against Feyenoord, Rotterdam. Supported by the chants of "Eye of the Tiger", his emergence was awe-inspiring. That song, played by the American rock band Survivor, was the title song of the film Rocky III. On 24th July 1982 the song climbed to the number one spot on the American hit list. Van Barneveld is passionate about music. He loves those whining guitars. Rock bands like AC/DC are his favourites. Raymond instinctively chose the "Eye of the Tiger", to be his intro number, accompanying him onto the stage. To remind the audience, that the sharp eye of the tiger never misses his goal.

In the opening party Raymond played Sean Palfrey. The dart player from Newport, Monmouthshire in Wales, had done very well the year before. Palfrey was only eliminated in the quarterfinal by Roland Scholten. The left-handed Welshman was no opponent for Raymond in 1999 though. He finished the game with an easy 3 sets to 0 win in the first round.

Two young Dutchmen, Co Stompé and Raymond van Barneveld, share a joke with a "Bobby" in England.

"Two friends of mine had the ADO team coloured scarf with them and suggested that I wear it. It seems to have become a bit of a tradition to make your celebration entries special ones, rather like in the days of the old Olympians I suppose. Initially I was a little sceptical, but I decided after some cajoling, to do it in the end. The resulting impact on my home patch was fantastic. I come from The Hague and follow ADO game by game. So in and around our city and at the football club itself, the people were cock-a-hoop."

The head turning "Return of the Legend" scarf entrance.

For the second round, Les Wallace was on the menu. Another southpaw player it turned out. With the eccentric Scotsman playing you, the result was never a foregone conclusion. He was a friendly type, who, on his day, could beat any player who stepped up on to the stage. As was the case in 1997, when he won *The Embassy*, coming from nowhere. In 1995, Les was beaten by Raymond in the first round. Now, four years on, he almost managed to take his revenge. Both men turned in an unforgettable performance on the day. It started straight away in the first set, as Raymond score climbed vertically, up to an unprecedented average of 40 points a dart. Even with the wind behind Raymond, it was still Wallace who snatched the set

in the end. The event was turning into a dogfight. Schoofs sat at one of the reserved tables, right in front of the stage and was shouting encouragement, the whole game. So much so, that he was horse in the end. He clutched a talisman in one hand and in the other he held a lucky coin. It must have worked, as Wallace wasted five throws that could, at that point, have clinched the game for him. Barney bounced back at the 11th hour of the game to win 3-2. The release of pent up tension in him was visible to the extreme. Tears started flowing and all around, his fans started joining in as well. The quarterfinal was next.

"It was during the second round of the 1999 Embassy, that I had my best vein of luck. What happened during that phase of the competition, was not an everyday occurrence. Seldom have I been so excited as during this game. Quite honestly, I thought I was dead and buried. I was playing like a man possessed during the final round but nothing seemed to be going my way. The Scot was hitting everything. Only at the end did he falter, luckily for me, I assure you. This downturn gave me the slenderest of chances, which I seized but I was lucky."

One of the most exciting games that Raymond ever took part in was during 1999, against Les Wallace. The Scot missed five game closing throws and Barney managed to win in the end. The following morning however, both players enjoyed a bubble bath and some champagne together.

His opponent in the quarterfinal was the Australian green keeper Steve Duke sr. A bearded Aussie and a likeable chap but for Raymond he would turn out to be no more than a parody character from his favourite TV series The Dukes of Hazard. "I'm gonna get that Duke boy", chuckled the young man from The Hague, an hour before the start of the match. His prediction came true. Performing to an audience of 2.2 million TV viewers in The Netherlands, he comfortably defeated his Australian opponent 5 sets to 1.

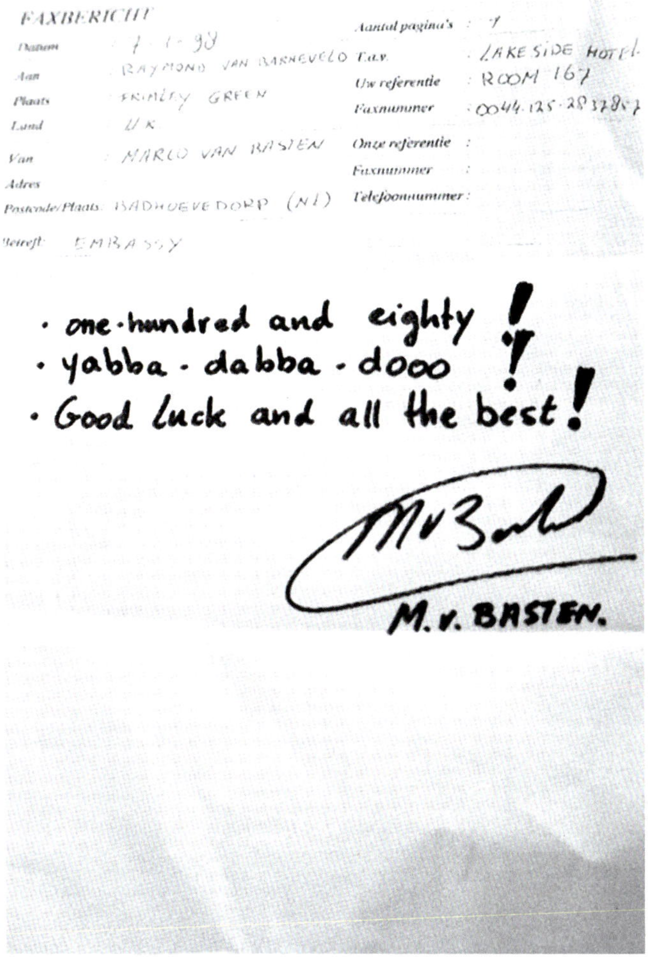
FAXBERICHT

Datum: 7-1-98
Aan: RAYMOND VAN BARNEVELD
Plaats: FRIMLEY GREEN
Land: UK
Van: MARCO VAN BASTEN
Adres:
Postcode/Plaats: BADHOEVEDORP (NL)
Betreft: EMBASSY

Aantal pagina's: 1
T.a.v.: LAKESIDE HOTEL
Uw referentie: ROOM 167
Faxnummer: 0044-125-2837857
Onze referentie:
Faxnummer:
Telefoonnummer:

· one-hundred and eighty!
· yabba-dabba-dooo!
· Good luck and all the best!

M.v. BASTEN.

A copy of the fax that Marco van Basten sent Raymond after his win in 1999.

"That morning I received a fax from Marco van Basten. It was a very thoughtful and friendly gesture. Back then, after every round you survived, there were faxes being pushed under the door of your hotel room. Van Basten had just hung up his football boots and had started playing a bit of golf. He was totally frustrated at having to stop playing football, so early in his career. He was avoiding the cameras and any publicity at the time. It was really kind that he made an exception for me and spoke highly of my achievement, when being interviewed by the Dutch TV station SBS6. I found this gesture very special. Soon after, I received a fax from him, in which he congratulated me and wished me luck for the next round.

The funny thing is that I had never even met him. I hope to one day though. Apart from Marco there are a few other Dutch celebs on my list that I would like to meet. One, as a football fan, would obviously be Johan Cruyff, but also his contemporary Johan Neeskens. Both of them were favourites of mine, back in the seventy's. Dennis Bergkamp is also on my wish list. All four of these Dutch footballers were internationally recognised players in their day. For me, they stood out as stars. I was fortunate enough however to meet The Hague's football legend Aad Mansveld, once or twice. He ran a sports shop on the Genestetlaan, close to my Lower Technical School. I used to go in there for a chat. I also met Willem van Hanegem a couple of times. He was another footballing hero of mine from the seventy's. Fast-forwarding to more recent generations of footballers, I was a huge fan of Gerald Vanenburg. I'm pleased to say that we have become very good friends.

I have also been able to meet several top English footballers. One of the nicest memories that I have, was when I met Michael Owen. The last round robin games in the PDC's Premier League were played on 1 May 2008, at the Metro Radio Arena in Newcastle. Players from Newcastle United, I think the entire team were invited and sat in the front row. Before the competition Michael Owen came up and we chatted for a while. He also threw some darts, belonging to several different players, including mine. Wayne Mardle did some exhibition stuff, by inventively, blowing his arrows at the board…and scoring!

Owen was shorter than I had imagined. We were preparing for a competition, so I wasn't able to speak to him for very long. At his request though, I explained to him the differences between each player's choice of darts. He seemed to throw okay, however I had already noticed that most British sportsmen were good at throwing darts. During the grand Slam of Darts there was a pro-celebrity tournament. I was chosen to play the doubles with the cricket player Phil Tufnell, a man who batted right handed and bowled with his left. He made a big racket when he got onto the stage and the public loved it. He also threw a decent arrow.

A PDC Premier League round robin was also played in April 2008 at the Wembley Arena, an indoor area which is situated opposite the Wembley stadium where *the holy grass* is worshiped every so often. I can remember that Dennis Bergkamp scored a wonderful goal there. He volleyed the ball straight over the keeper and into the net. I also remember England's defeat at the hands of the Dutch during Euro 96.

A meeting like that with Owen was really enjoyable. I love English football and follow all the clubs with Dutch players in them, enthusiastically. Once I was invited to go to Chelsea, when Robben was playing there.

Raymond, the football fan together with Michael Owen, the darts fan.

They showed me the Premier League Trophy, which Chelsea had won. After I had put on a pair of white gloves, I was allowed to hold it for a photo. Magnificent! A few months later I went to the Manchester United ground and once again, was allowed to hold a ManU icon for a photo. I was also given a guided tour around the stadium. The thing that hit home most was that there were still fresh flowers being laid for The Busby Babes who died in the 1958 Munich-Riem airport disaster. Can you imagine, it happened more than fifty years ago!

We don't have these deep felt sporting traditions in The Netherlands. They would have stopped commemorating such an event long ago, I think. I notice that I'm also more respected, based on my darting achievements, in England. In The Netherlands I don't hold the same level of respect. As soon as I set foot on English soil I am classed as an 8-fold world champion (including the 3 world cups). Full stop. The same goes for dart, cricket, rugby or football players, etc. Sportsmen who have achieved something, are treated with the respect they deserve. This also applies to the legendary football clubs themselves and England has a lot of those too, including the likes of Spurs, ManU and Liverpool, not to mention the cup giant killers, Norwich City and so on.

All the famous English clubs have an incredible history, a wonderful here and now and an even brighter future. So I could never be a fan of just one club. Individually though, footballers like Tottenham's Glen Hoddle, Owen and Shearer are my favourite stars. As with football, it is the same with darts, the words 'Premier League' identify the most exciting competition in the world."

The more Raymond fought his way through each round of the '99 Embassy, the more, the mainly English opposition riled against him. They thought he lacked a certain sportsmanship, was too much of a loner. Of course they were also wary of the talented Dutchman's threat of winning their tournament, for the second year in a row. This darting cold war, between the predominantly English opposition and the Dutch, reached its peak on the final Saturday of the tournament. Semi-finalist Ronnie Baxter refused to agree with the interchange of the 2 semi finals. Dutch TV channel SBS6 made a late request, wanting Raymond to play during Dutch prime time. The BDO was prepared to agree to this but Baxter wouldn't. He sited the official draw, which stated that the match between Raymond and Chris Mason was set to be played first. He didn't want to have anything to do with satisfying the cravings of the Dutch TV audience.

"The darts world in general is very sporting. I know I'm not that sporting though, especially when I lose. It's just unacceptable to me. Maybe this is why some of the other boys find me a bit unusual but it's okay, I understand where they're coming from. If other guys in the competition favour sitting in the bar until 4 in the morning its fine by me but don't count me in. I like going to bed early, certainly if I'm playing an important match the following day. Maybe it's just that I've managed to put their nose out of joint, being a rookie Dutchman, walking in and then walking off with their tournament trophy. Of course it's not nice for the locals, I can understand that."

Raymond also has friends outside the darts world: Former Dutch international footballer Gerald Vanenburg is one.

1999: Raymond can't believe that he has just beaten Ronnie Baxter in the final. He's won The Embassy again!

Raymond, now in the semi final, came up against Chris Mason. The English enfant terrible had won the quarterfinal by beating Martin Adams in a great, maybe all time best game. Mason won 5-4 at the death, after lagging way behind, pulling back from 1-4 down, late on.

That evening Mason celebrated his victory by ordering the mandatory round of drinks at the bar...His wife (at the time) was pregnant. She had been overcome with excitement during his game and didn't feel too good. She wanted to go to a local hospital, to get checked out. Chris wanted to accompany her but he had some other things on his mind too. This eventually resulted in a steaming row. In the end Mason was told to leave his hotel room, by his wife. He spent that night sleeping on the floor in the referee's room. By the time he had to play Raymond the following day the Englishman seemed to have recovered from the event but just how much this influenced his tournament we will never known.

Lisa Mason, who was pregnant, got so excited during husband Chris's quarterfinal match that she started to feel ill. She wanted to go to the hospital after the game. This seemed to have caused quite a quarrel between Lisa and Chris, later that evening.

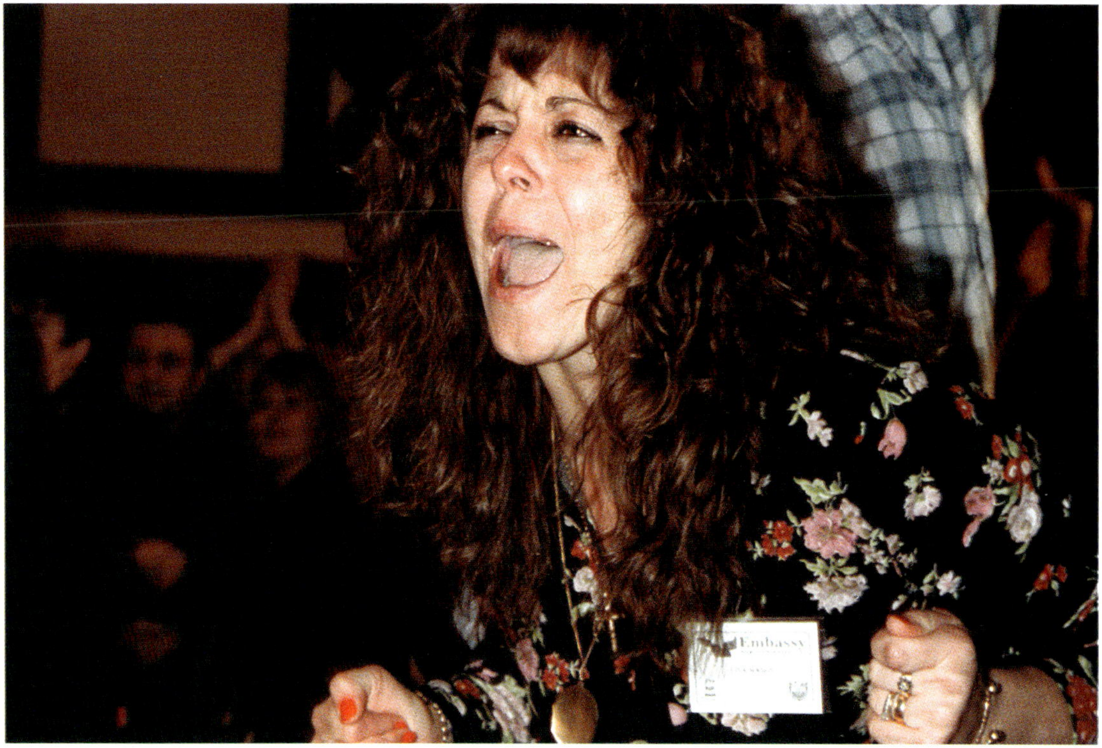

He was certainly not strong enough to keep up with the Dutchman, who shrugged off his competitor 5-2 in a best of 9 sets duel. Raymond, now brimming with confidence, readied himself for the final. Ronnie Baxter, nicknamed "The Rocket", was to be his opponent. The Englishman was strongly supported by all his dart-playing mates. The pressure on him to bring the title back to England was enormous. The smear campaign aimed at Barney was starting to get a little worn. The public, mostly English, were united in their support for their fellow countryman on that Sunday the 10th January. Unfortunately for him this situation was spot-on for Raymond. He normally performed at his best under this kind of pressure. He focused on imagining the hyped up English dart players, coupled with perhaps as many as 1200 supporters, to be his archenemies for the game.

The attitude of both profs resulted in a blood curdling game. Both players ended up running into difficulties. After four sets Raymond was 1-3 down. Then the man from The Hague won three sets in a row, powering to a sets lead of 4 to 3. Then, another comeback, this time from Baxter. He won each of the following two sets 3 legs to 0. The small Dutch group in the audience held their breath. Raymond won the tenth set by the same margin 3 legs to 0 and so made it all square, at 5 sets all. Just the same as a year earlier, in 1998, they had to play an eleventh and deciding set to find the winner. His back to the wall, Raymond managed to perform once again and prove that *he was the man*. He managed to hold his nerve and followed through at the critical moment with a finish on double 16, so winning this vital set, 4 legs to 2. His reward, a second Embassy title in a row.

"I ended my speech with a one liner, a quip 'The postman always wins twice', as a play on the title to the film *The postman always rings twice*. That raised a laugh from all the guests. This time I was a lot less nervous during making my speech, because I had survived making the previous one, no doubt."

The Netherlands watched the final, *en masse*. SBS6 scored a new record with the number of viewers recorded watching. The entire country was gripped by darts fever again and was captivated by Raymond van Barneveld's, repeated personal success. His homecoming turned into an even greater and more exciting event than the previous year.

Helen Hofland, former director of the Dutch Darts Bond, remembers his arrival at Schiphol well: "Raymond and I flew back into Amsterdam together. After we landed we casually walked out of the arrivals area. Suddenly we were inundated with questions from the press, who had decided to forward charge! All we could hear and see was the clicking of cameras and flashlights going off. People were pushing, pulling and even thumping each other to get a better view of the action. I had seen this kind of stuff in films but we were right in the middle of it then. The only thing Raymond was able to murmur was: 'Help!' He turned round and gave me the trophy, then tried to protect himself as best he could. I managed to organise a press area to be set up, after speaking with a ground stewardess. They all filed in there, swiftly. A new challenge dawned. For the first time in his life Raymond had to give a full-on press conference. This proved to be a very difficult moment for him. He was literally being thrown to the wolves and was totally unprepared for this kind of reception. Added to this, he only had one thing on his mind and that was to see Silvia and the children. That only happened after the very last question. As we walked out of the conference room towards the exit, a second wave of interest engulfed us. At the moment we opened the doors, Raymond said something like: 'Helen, what's going on here?' There was another mass of people waiting to see him. This was indeed a reflection of what was about to happen concerning the importance of darts, up and down the country but at that moment we didn't realise that. It was really manic there, crazy. We were expecting some people yes, but nothing like that. It took quite a while before he arrived home."

"What really overwhelmed me was the reception I received when I arrived back in The Netherlands. I will never forget it. From the very moment that the sliding doors exit at Schiphol opened up it was mayhem, utter mayhem. The Marechaussee, the Dutch military police tried to ensure we could walk through safely. It was then that I thought, I was really glad I hadn't allowed my children to come to Schiphol to meet me. I immediately thought of the Heysel* football stadium disaster. If someone had fallen over they could have easily been trampled on. It was just terrifying. I felt like some kind of pop star. It seemed just as much of a madhouse as it must have been with *Oranje*, The Dutch national Football team, in 1988 when they arrived home after winning the European Championship. People with scarves ran alongside the car as we left. Others drove behind us hooting as we made our way back to The Hague.

Barney raises the trophy in one hand and a bottle of champagne in the other. He's done his part. A good day at the office!

* Footnote from the writers. The Heysel disaster took place on the 29th May 1985, before the European Cup Final between Liverpool (England) and Juventus (Italy), at the Heysel stadium in Brussels. During the match, 39 supporters (32 Italians) died and at least 200 people were seriously injured.

The final was watched by almost four million viewers on the TV. From that day onward I've never been able to cross the road without being recognised. I'm still extremely proud of the fact that I helped to put darts on the Dutch map this way. It's proved itself to be a fun and thrilling spectator sport and many people have started playing themselves. Children, especially, have taken to the sport very positively. I love children. A photo here, a signature there, I've always got time for them. I see it as a bonus. Even when it is not convenient. With adults it's different, I think. I expect them to let me eat in peace when I'm having a meal in a restaurant. But if I say anything, you're immediately labelled as arrogant. Even though I'm just like any other person, trying to get a bite to eat. That's not much fun. Since 1999, it seems I have not been allowed to say NO to anyone, I became public property instantly. This of course took a lot of getting used to.

A few weeks after the final in '99 I was interviewed by an English newspaper. They asked me among other things, how popular I had now become in The Netherlands. For example could I be compared to Cruyff and Van Basten? As four million people had recently watched the final, I said that the entire population knew who I was, just like everyone knew who these two footballers were. What do you know? They gleefully wrote that I saw myself as the third best know sports star in The Netherlands. In The Netherlands this was also taken completely out of context. Of course I didn't see myself in this way at all. What I did find funny was the phrase Martin Adams always used, to compare his standing to that of a professional footballer. If they asked him, he would say that yes, he had more world titles to his name than David Beckham would ever amass but that Beckham was still the multi-millionaire.

I also received a postcard from Louis van Gaal, on behalf of the FC Barcelona management and team, in 1999. He had taken time off from training especially, to see me play the final. That year too, Van Gaal had identified me as a role model of concentration, perfection and persistence. All the boys at FC Barcelona were extremely happy for me when I won the final. That's amazing. Even people you wouldn't immediately associate with the game like Van Gaal, watch darts. Likewise, Dutch comedian André van Duin, star footballer Phillip Cocu, etc. I've received emails from them all. I am very down to earth when it comes to mixing with any famous Dutch personalities. I appreciate what they do in life, but I don't normally go so far as asking for a signature or a photo with them. What I do look at, is how they deal with fame. I must admit, it took a bit of getting used to, when these famous people told me they enjoyed watching me play darts.

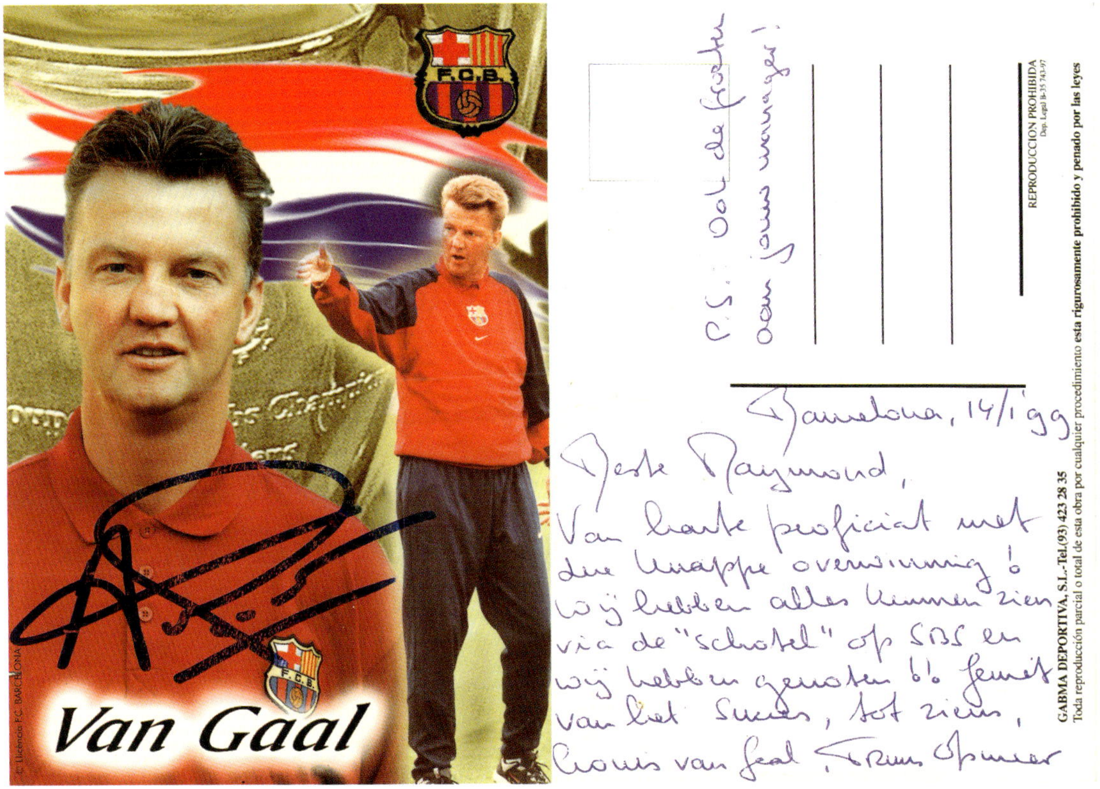

On the 14th January 1999 this picture postcard came through our letterbox. Written on it was a personal message from Louis van Gaal, on behalf of the FC Barcelona team, where he was the manager at the time.

Two days after my return to The Netherlands I was appointed by the ADO Den Haag football club, at their stadium in the Zuiderpark, The Hague to be the club's ambassador. I received a shirt with the number 180 on the back and a season ticket for life. 'What's happening?' I asked myself. All this just because of getting on the stage before the final, wearing a green and yellow scarf with 'Return of the Legend' written on it. Just a few days later I was made a Freeman of the city of The Hague. I couldn't make it all up if I tried. I was only the ninth person ever, to have such an honour bestowed on them. I never even dreamed that something as fantastic as this could happen to me. Everyone else knew it was going to happen, except me. I didn't even know what it meant, an honorary citizenship? I still don't really know. What exactly can I do with this title, I wonder? If I park my car illegally somewhere, would I still receive a fine? From a practical standpoint the award doesn't really mean that much to me but nevertheless I'm still very proud of having been given it.

The Van Barneveld's show off The Embassy cup to the thousands of people gathered in The Hague's Town Hall Atrium. Raymond had also just been made a Freeman of the city of The Hague.

On 25th January I received The Hague's sports trophy, presented to me by Marco Borsato, a popular Dutch singer. It was a cash prize to the tune of Dfl 5.000 that I handed over to three charities, including War Child and the Ronald McDonald Children's fund. Marco was extremely enthusiastic, as he also actively supports Warchild. I had met him a couple of times before, for instance in 1995 when we were on the Ivo Niehe *TV-show*. Every time he saw me he would throw his arm round me and we would speak for ages. A different world you know. So at the moment I am the flavour of the month, I'm popular, meaning I'm approached by them as if they have known me for years. It's easy to start thinking: 'Yes, well, sorry, but I don't know how you guys treat each other and I don't know you. I am Raymond van Barneveld and yes, I can throw a dart or two quite well, but not much else.' When I was on the TV-show in '95 I brought along a set of darts for Borsato as a gift. The nice thing was that he responded quickly afterwards. Two weeks later I received a signed CD from him in the post: 'Dreams do come true, greetings Marco.' 'Very nice', I thought. He didn't have to do that. If I promise something I commit myself 100%. Obviously he thinks this way too. We have the same background. He also went through the LTS stream. Maybe that's one reason why we get on so well. When we see each other, we always have a laugh. Marco Borsato does not put it on; he's just naturally a great guy.

Two Dutch celebrities stand together as friends in the spotlight: Marco Borsato and Raymond. The dart-playing maestro is pictured presenting some of the money from an award he received to the Warchild Association, of which the singer is an ambassador.

Speaking of singers. I will never forget the get-together I had in 2007 with Engelbert Humperdinck. I was called up in June of that year by someone from *The Toppers*. The 'Toppers' consist of three popular Dutch male singers who perform in a series of concerts in the Amsterdam ArenA, once a year. That year they had Engelbert Humperdinck involved in the concert and they were interested to know if I wanted to come to the Arena to meet him.

He had a dartboard put up in his dressing room, it was a prerequisite in his contract, part of his rider and they said that he wanted to play a leg with me. Initially I thought that it was a set-up by a radio or television programme, so I was very careful what I said. I played along and asked him if Tom Jones would also be singing. But they maintained that it was true about Engelbert. So, one Saturday I went to the ArenA with my children and some other family members. We were shown around the stadium by René Froger, one of the three singers. The children found it really amazing. My mom and mother in law nearly fainted when they met Engelbert, as they used to dance along to his songs, in earlier days. Engelbert and I threw a few legs together and he played very well. He was actually quite good at the game. In between, he told me that he remembered having dinner with Elvis. Then he confided in me that he only had one idol and that was Raymond van Barneveld. That was a bit too much to take in. Even if I still doubted it, he seemed to be enjoying my company and was generally having a great time. At one point he asked me if I could play golf. I replied honestly that I was not very good at it, but he still invited me to play a round with him, the following day in Noordwijk. So there we were, René Froger, Engelbert, the girls and I. We spent the day out golfing. Afterwards we had a delicious meal and exchanged some super stories. He has performed with all the great names and could share a tale or two. It really was a wonderful experience. He also gave me his phone number but I'm not someone who goes around phoning people out of the blue.

The following is a tale of my time in the TV spotlight. It took place under the guidance of Willibrord Frequin a Dutch TV personality. I took part in *Toppers*, a Dutch television programme, with him. What an experience that was! It was filmed over a couple of days. It turned out to be an extremely exciting weekend. Each morning at six I was picked up and driven to Maastricht, to a health spa.

While we were filming sometimes things didn't go very well. Hmm, well, with Willibrord in charge nothing was allowed to go wrong. He was not that easy to work with, a perfectionist. I didn't have a problem with that but it wasn't always easy for his colleagues. He's a first class professional, who manages to notice everything.

During filming I went to visit a girl who was suffering from cancer. She was very ill and only had a few months left to live. She was also a fan of mine and I was very fortunate to be able to make a surprise visit to see her. She had baked a cake for me and had also created some drawings. I gave her a special set of darts as a gift. A few months later we heard she had passed away. That was terrible news and was difficult to accept.

Raymond in the ADO's Zuiderpark football stadium in The Hague, kicking a ball around with Willibrord Frequin.

Something similar happened to me during the 1999 Embassy. A few Englishmen came up to me with a request to sign a card for a young boy who was terminally ill. This was in the player's lounge section of the hotel. They told me that he was a big fan of mine and that he didn't have very long to live. He was already too ill to come to the tournament. I felt very sorry for him. You see, I feel the pain of others when they are suffering, especially where children are concerned. So I sent him the signed card, together with a set of darts and one of my playing shirts.

Literally the high point of all the festivities after the '99 win, was being invited to fly in a Dutch Royal Air Force, F16 fighter jet. I jumped at the chance, I wouldn't have wanted to miss it for the world, an absolutely unique experience. How they managed to squeeze me into the cockpit, I don't know to this day. I was quite big at the time and the largest suit they had, barely fitted me. As a young boy I had posters of planes all over my wall, I even built model planes. I had a briefing first before the flight, with a lieutenant. If anything went wrong I would have to eject and use the parachute to get down. I went a little quiet at this thought but still went up. The pilot did his whole routine in the air. The pressure was so great that I didn't have normal control over my body anymore. So I sat there, almost wetting my pants. Luckily that didn't actually happen, as it wouldn't have looked very good when I got out!

When I stepped out of the fighter I felt woozy. I wasn't scared though. Straight up, then headlong thousands of metres down, followed by a loop. I thought it was great. It was just like experiencing a thousand fairground rides, compressed into a tiny space of six square feet.

The all time high of the festivities after Barney's second Embassy win: A flight as a co-pilot in a F16-fighter jet.

The accolades just didn't seem to stop. At the beginning of March, in Creil, North of Emmeloord, a tulip was named after me. It was planted there. The same evening, in Aalsmeer I presented an Edison, a Dutch music award, to the Golden Earring, a band who made the song *Radar Love* famous. It was a lifetime achievement award, a magnificent prize. Great guys. I knew them already, as they are also from The Hague. They promised me a ticket to one of their shows in the area sometime. I'm still waiting…

In Amsterdam I threw a few darts with Jerry Springer at the SBS6 studio. I spoke to him for a while. He said that he knew me, but I'm not sure that he did. Springer in real life is not very tall. I never watched his shows Who the hell is Jerry Springer? I don't like his programmes. People getting angry with each other on the stage, no thanks.

In-between all the commotion the dart tournaments still went on. One of my best performances ever, was at the Spring Cup of '99. An annual event, at which, seven teams from different countries, consisting of eight men and four women each, play against each other. I played 98 legs over the whole day, of which 49 were played as singles. During that time I won 88 of them.

Incredible! The Dutch team won the Spring Cup. A day later I beat Co Stompé* in the singles final. I did need two class finishes though, of 156 and 121 in order to beat him. That was an important victory for me.

On April 7th, I thought the world had gone mad. It was the first in a series, called: *Barney's darts show*. I had my own darts show on television. We signed a deal for a run of 26 programmes with Joop van den Ende, a famous Dutch theatre producer. I had thought of a great formula for the show but they didn't want to listen to me. After two pilot programmes the format was modified. Unfortunately it didn't work out. I wasn't so happy they stopped everything in mid-stream either. I still think there is a target group out there that would be interested in a darts quiz. You must of course be able to give out good quality prizes, like holidays for example. I remember in the 90's there was a programme called *Bull's Eye* in England. That was a big hit, very popular. Three couples were throwing for prizes. In the end *Barney's darts show* was taken off the air, after fifteen broadcasts. It didn't work out in The Netherlands. The viewing figures were to low to continue. Master of Ceremonies,** Caller, scorer and referee Martin Fitzmaurice, famous for his 'one hundred and eighty' announcements, actioned a court case against Chiel van Praag. Back then Chiel was still the boss of my manager, Ad Schoofs. The quiz had, according to Mr. Fitzmaurice, used his voice illegally. The eleven remaining broadcasts were supposed to be filled by a docu-soap series about my day-to-day life. I was not very happy with that. During preparations for tournaments our lives are very quite. Besides, how do you fill an hour of TV time, for eleven whole weeks, with the daily events in Raymond van Barneveld's life. It wasn't really on now, was it?

* Footnote from the writers: Co Stompé, a dart player, born and bred in Amsterdam is well known for his humour on and off the stage. Before he became a professional dart player he was a tram driver. Stompé became European Champion in 1998, won the Spring Cup twice and has been allowed to call himself Dutch Champion three times so far.

** Footnote from the writers: A Master Caller (BDO) or Master of Ceremonies (PDC) is the person who calls the dart players onto the stage and also announces their departure.

As if things were not crazy enough, there was also a surprise party organised for me on 20 April for my 32nd birthday. I had thrown a double 16 in life by turning 32. I had no idea of what was going on. It turned out to be a great party with family, friends and lots of other people.

Guus Meeuwis the singer performed, as well as comedian Jeroen Smits. There were even dance acts. Later that evening I was given a Nissan Maxima as a present. Including a route planner! An unforgettable day that was also really relaxing and quite a lot of fun too. It does take a little getting used to when everyone forms a line, waiting to kiss you. It was also quite a job to ferry all the presents back home. Meeuwis and I had a lot of fun and he performed for free, just as a friend with his group, Vagant.

Raymond singing at his 32nd birthday together with Guus Meeuwis and Vagant.

Okay, a lot had happened but that's not where it ended, at all. On 30th April 1999 Silvia ushered me along to the Ministry of Social Affairs. It turned out I was to be decorated with a Dutch recognition of achievement. Ridder in de Order van Orange Nassau, a Dutch knighthood. I didn't know anything about it! To my surprise, my parents, parents in-laws and a delegation of the Dutch Darts Federation were already there waiting for the presentation. What a wonderful surprise and an honour! I dare to say, in all modesty that this was the most incredible recognition I have ever received. State Secretary Margo Vliegenthart began her speech: 'It is Her Majesty's pleasure to…' After this intro my mind stopped functioning properly. I didn't hear another word. Wow, on behalf of the Queen. There could be no greater recognition. Winning *The Embassy* four times, together with securing the Ladbrokes once is one thing but when Her Majesty Queen Beatrix showed her appreciation for what I had managed to achieve for darts in The Netherlands, that made for indescribable feelings. Knight of the order of Oranje Nassau is my exact title. I have used this accolade as a source of strength constantly, even to this day. I was very emotional about receiving it at the time. In England, Eric Bristow has been made an MBE, a Member of the Order of the British Empire. We are the only two dart players in the world that carry a royal title."

State Secretary Margo Vliegenthart attaching the Royal insignia to Raymond's lapel in 1999. The title was given in recognition of his achievements, soon after his second win at The Embassy in England.

Superstition also plays a very important role in Raymond's life. A fortune cookie from Gallant Restaurant in Frimley, a long-standing favourite of Barney's, foretold of what he could expect in 1999 and it came true!

Superstition

Despite all the partying, there was still a lot of darts to be played. Everyone expected the reigning Embassy World Champion to be able to win just about anything, but it wasn't that easy. Raymond wanted to win specific tournaments, if not for himself, then for others.

"It was extremely important for me to win the first Brandstaff Masters title. After all, they were my main sponsor and in The Netherlands, everyone assumed that I would win the tournament in Veldhoven. All of the world's top players were there. Of course that attracted spectators. I was really quite relieved that I was able to beat them all. It was a good tournament and it became the precursor for the great Dutch Grand Slam tournaments.

Jenneke Sonneveld was the director of Brandstaff. She is a wonderful person. Along with Joop van Odenhoven, who took care of the marketing, she managed the company. I owe a lot to these people. I still see them from time to time, which does me good. We worked until the end of our three-year contract but it was not extended, because Jenneke got a bit carried away with the Brandstaff Masters. It had cost quite a bit of money and her superiors held her accountable. Her successor did not appreciate darts very much, so it was logical that there wouldn't be a follow-up contract. It was just a pity that they waited so long to tell me and it played on my mind during the 2000 Embassy. It was contractually determined that they would let me know after the tournament and I was worried about my annual income. There were already a few indications that they wanted to end the contract. They eventually asked us if they could buy it out and if we knew of another sponsor. Try finding one of those! I would have preferred them to tell me before *The Embassy*, that they were ending it. Now I was under even more pressure, which caused a distraction that I really didn't need. I hoped that performing well would influence their decision in my favour."

The friction between the English on the one hand and the Dutch organisation, together with Raymond on the other, was also noticeable in Veldhoven. There were many complaints and Raymond's English opponents were a bit anti, even though it was thanks to him that they could earn quite a bit of extra money in The Netherlands. Raymond remained undaunted. After his victory, he celebrated by going camping in the vicinity of Roosendaal and was back for the Belgium Open on 1st August.

"I really didn't want to go there. I had more than enough points for the world rankings, but I was talked into it by Ad. The Belgium Open is just as difficult as, for example, the Dutch Open, even though significantly less people take part. However, by viewing it more as a training event, it turned into becoming a great tournament for me. I won, mainly thanks to Ad. He was resolute. He wanted me to go and to win. Ad was the kind of person who would oppose me and not go along with everything I said. That was definitely the best way to deal with me."

1999 was the best year of his career. Raymond maintained his no. 1 position in the world rankings, with a record 52 points. It was a unique achievement, as only the six best results counted. A victory in all other international open tournaments delivers 8 points but his win at *The Embassy* yielded 12, resulting in him securing the maximum total of 52. Everything was going wonderfully and Raymond was very happy with himself. He was a professional who was earning good money and performing to the best of his ability... Until, that is, a slip one evening at a party, threw a spanner in the works.

"Wherever I went, I always made it to the semi-finals, in spite of the fact that I was extremely busy. There was even a period when I didn't want to do anything. I remember thinking 'Do I really have to go to the Danish open again?' But I kept going, which was good. It made me feel great, because I knew that I would improve as a result. The truth is, I'm a lazy person. I would much rather earn money by sitting at a computer. I never want to give it my all, because I'm afraid of what might happen if things were to go wrong. And they did, at a very unexpected moment. At the end of August, while in Majorca. Up until that point, I had been living a dream. Everything I had touched had turned to gold.

Ad Schoofs had contacted Jan Bakker from the Veronica disco in Majorca and arranged for me to go there for a week, in August. Dutch artists always performed there in the summer and the idea of these artists playing darts against Barney appealed to them. The tickets were paid for and we received a little pocket money. All I had to do was to play darts from 2.30pm to 3.00 am. On the last evening however, I'd had enough of drinking only water and 7 UP, so I decided to drink Bacardi and cokes all night. I met a group from The Hague and we started doing crazy moves on the dance floor. At a certain point 'Oh, Oh, The Hague' could be heard from the speakers. When the number ended, everyone carried on jumping around. Suddenly, one person slipped and pulled the rest down with him. I also fell and felt a pain shoot straight through my ankle. Nevertheless, we took a taxi to the hotel for a short night's sleep, flew to Dusseldorf the next morning and drove from there back to The Hague.

I was in so much pain that Ad started to worry. In Germany, I had to be transported in a wheelchair and once we arrived in The Hague, we went straight to the Westeinde Ziekenhuis (hospital). Here, they established that my ankle was broken and it was eventually put in a cast. The worst part was that I never usually party. A world champion should be allowed to do that once in a while though, right? I was having a great time, yet with my luck, something like this was inevitable. We told the press that I'd fallen down a flight of stairs. If I'd have told them what had really happened, it might have cost me sponsors and lead to negative publicity. I'd already had enough unpleasant experiences of that nature by then.

The ankle fracture couldn't have happened at a worse time, as it was very near the WC in Durban and The Match of the Century against Phil Taylor. The latter of these was planned for November at the Wembley Arena and I was definitely not looking forward to it.

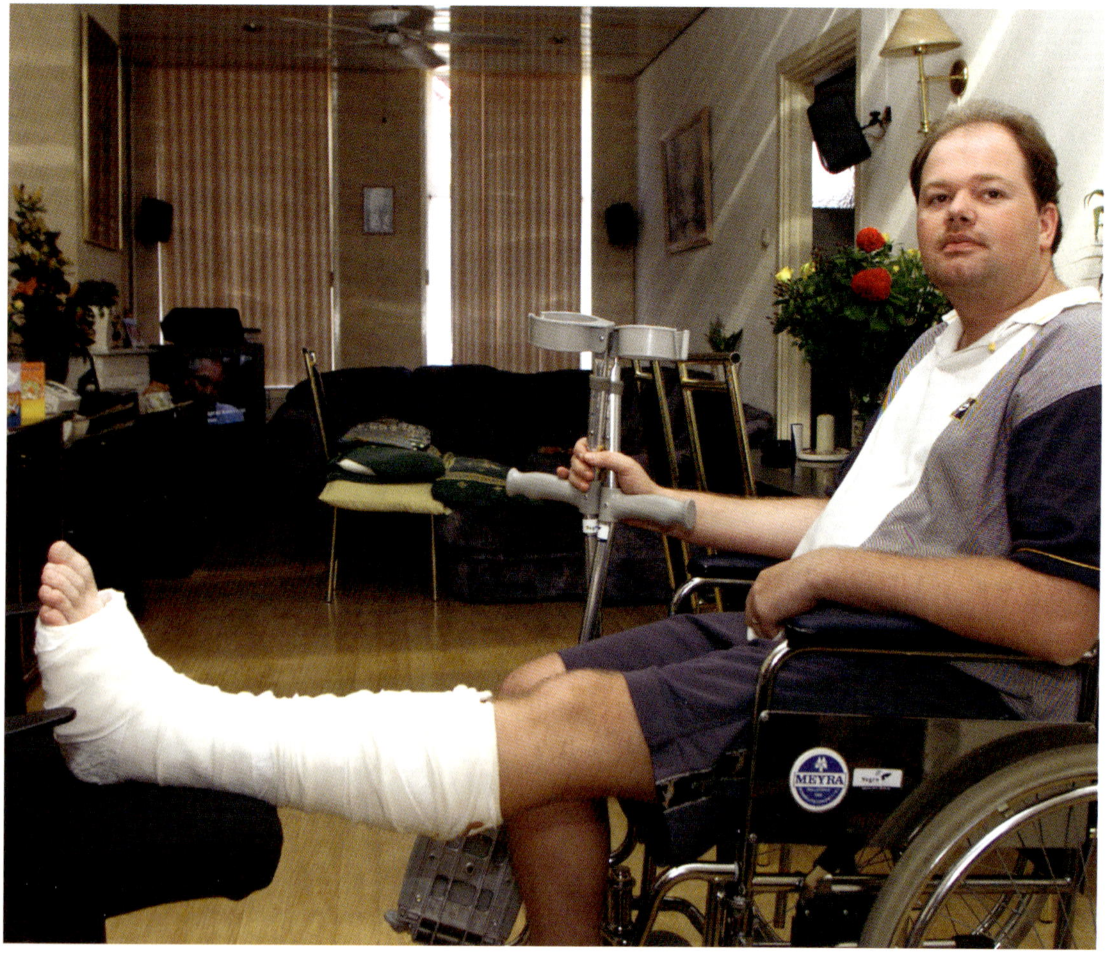

Raymond broke his left ankle on a working holiday in Majorca. The cast was removed a week early, so that he could take part in the WC in Durban. It was here that Barney became world champion in 1999. (Photo: Edwin Smulders.)

My rehabilitation was a slow process. Every day I had to lift myself, step-by-step, backwards, up to my apartment in IJsselstraat. The sweat would pour from my face but I was furious and that fury motivated me a lot. I was thinking 'I'm the one in pain now, but it'll be your turn soon.'

The cast was removed on a Friday afternoon and I flew to Durban on the following Tuesday. It was removed a week prematurely, as it was only supposed to come off three days after my departure for South Africa. I gave a cake to the staff at the hospital to thank them for their excellent care. My ankle probably didn't heal properly, as it still bothers me from time to time. Luckily it was my left ankle and not the leg I stand on to play darts. Otherwise it would have caused me a lot more trouble.

On Saturday, I won the official World Darts Federation world title. The WDF is the master organisation under which the BDO operates. Durban is a terrible city. In the hotel I was told about which streets not to go down if I wanted to survive. Small children begging for money. It was just awful. I wasn't allowed to wear any jewellery but my Barney chain went everywhere with me. I never take it off and with good reason. It definitely helped me to get through that World Championship too.

Superstition plays a significant role in Raymond's life, such as his habit of rubbing his Barney chain during a tense duel. This can be seen here during the sensational semi-final of the 2004 Lakeside Darts World Championship against Andy Fordham.

Wearing this chain is one of the superstitions I have had in the last few years. It could well be fed by my lack of self-confidence, yet I wasn't the one who started it. Tobie van Laarhoven gave me a five-cent coin before the first round of *The Embassy* in 1998. He said that I would get another one before each subsequent round. I asked him why and he said that it was purely for fun. At a certain point I had four coins, but he ran out before the final was set to take place. Whatever else happened, he had to find another coin for me. I think he travelled halfway across England to find a Dutch five-cent piece. We laughed about it a lot after I won the final, but it was the start of a series of attributes and rituals. From the ADO scarf, to touching the triple 20. I once mentioned my problem with self-esteem to astrologer Tineke de Caluwé. She had all kinds of advice and predictions. Obviously, I was keen to know how I would do against Phil Taylor in 1999. She said that she saw only good things ahead and did not foresee any problems. He would not succeed against me, she said. Well that didn't happen, did it. People like that always hide behind the fact that they cannot see a specific time. I find this a bit too convenient. If I were to phone her now, she would probably say: 'You see, you have beaten him a couple of times now. I must have seen one of those times back then.' I haven't visited her since, as I can't draw any strength from things like that. I lost to Phil 21-10. I suppose I was just looking for assurance all the time.

I also had a photo of my aunt Greet in my breast pocket. Aunt Greet was Silvia's aunt, who celebrated her birthday during our first date. The poor woman was very ill and the odd thing about it was, that I had more contact with her when she was ill, than I did prior to her illness. I spoke about her once to Dennis van Onselen, the coach of the Dutch team. He had gained quite a lot of insight into such matters as a result of his work. He told me that we had to spend the time we still had together wisely. I followed his advice and took her to places like Euro Disney, which she really enjoyed. On 20th November 1998, my father-in-law's birthday, she looked very ill. At that time my in-laws were teasing me about how I would lose my world title but aunt Greet responded immediately with: 'No Raymond, everything will be fine.' After this her condition worsened and I watched as the life drained from her. Only a few strands remained of what had once been a lovely head of hair. It was terrible. At the end Silvia and I were with her in the hospital, together with her husband Joop. We then decided that we had to stop her agony. Nobody deserves to be that ill and certainly not aunt Greet. You're suddenly confronted by the hard facts of life. It's a terrible blow for anyone and it upset me a lot. I carried her photo with me as a source of strength during the 1999 Embassy. I also dedicated this title to her. Later, I carried with me photos of my friend Albert Vroegop, who passed away much too early and of the children.

The superstitions became ever stranger. I carried stones, had magnets on my wrists, my chain around my neck, and so on. I tried everything to improve my self-confidence. It started to get ridiculous, because at the end of the day, only I could make it happen. Even so, the insecurity I had felt since childhood sometimes drove me crazy. I also wanted to stop drinking. Not that I drank too much but I did try alternative solutions like plasters, haptonomy, meditation and acupuncture to help me to relax, in the hope that I would no longer need a Bacardi and coke before matches. That's always been my aim, but I still haven't been able to achieve it. I'm in the spotlight at every tournament. There is too much at stake. If I had five million euros in the bank, I wouldn't have to worry about the end of my career. But I still haven't earned that much. That's why it's easy for a man like Phil Taylor to say that I should just try playing once without having had a drink. He's been financially independent for a couple of years now. He's one step ahead of me in that respect. So, I still have a drink and I still need external factors like superstition. That's just the way it is."

For years, Raymond carried this photo frame with him to every tournament. It contains photos of his children and his best friend Albert Vroegop.

Ad Schoofs also knows about diversity where it concerns forms of superstition. "Raymond's superstitions characterise his lack of confidence", analyses the man from Brabant. "He has to have something which he thinks will bring him luck or make him relax. I've always gone along with it. I always say: 'If a footballer thinks that pink shoelaces will make him score in every game, then he should lace his boots with pink shoelaces.' The most famous example of Raymond's superstitious nature, was kissing his pendant, which hung on a chain round his neck. The pendant was in the form of Barney Rubble from the Flintstones. He once snapped the chain into pieces, throwing it down the toilet in *The Embassy* VIP room after losing a match. I managed to find the pendant, but not the chain.

Raymond also consulted Henk de Gier, a seer and hypnotist from Leidschendam. He did benefit on this occasion, however. He also went to an acupuncturist and still uses the services of Marco van Gorp, a haptonomist from Rotterdam. What was remarkable about these events was the absolute trust that Raymond had in all of these people. That was until he lost a couple of times. Then they were to blame. It took an awful lot of effort to convince him that you can't always win – no matter how good you are – and that you shouldn't doubt yourself if you do lose. Raymond is just someone who needs something to hold on to. His diets are also an example of this. He's always trying out new ways to lose weight, from a blood diet, which involved adjusting his diet on the basis of blood test results, to training with ADO The Hague. Two aspects of Raymond's character converge in these diets. On the one hand, the lack of self confidence that makes him want to diet, and on the other, the lack of self discipline that prevents him from ever sticking to a diet for long."

Raymond kissing a photo of his aunt Greet.

If there is one thing Raymond is proud of, it's his Dutch heritage. He's a Dutchman through and through, and a fan of both Dutch hotchpotch food and football. He also likes to fly the red, white and blue, as can be seen here during the 2007 Masters of Darts. How different it was in 1999, after his defeat at the hand of Taylor.

Wembley

Owing to his many trophies and as a result of his Embassy title wins in particular, by 1999 Raymond had also achieved fame in England. In The Netherlands, the man from The Hague was considered the best dart player in the world. In England however, they thought they knew better. The best player in the world, as far as they were concerned was of course 'their' Phil Taylor. In The Netherlands, Phil was known only to very well informed darts followers. Back then, PDC tournaments were not aired on television and for the Dutch, there was only one tournament: The Embassy. In November 1999, a spectacular match was organised between the English and Dutch champions. In the run-up to the tournament, Raymond feared the worst – and quite rightly so. He wasn't enjoying himself, his self-confidence was slipping like sand through his fingers. He faltered, losing the duel 21-10. In actual fact however, he lost a lot more than just the competition.

"The initiative for the match against Phil Taylor at Wembley Arena in 1999 was taken by PDC boss Barry Hearn. After I had won *The Embassy* for the second time, Phil wanted to pit himself against me. The first competition offered was based on all or nothing. The winner would receive 100,000 British pounds, the loser nothing. We didn't accept it of course. We wanted to split it fifty-fifty, but eventually we settled for 60-40.

During the first negotiations there was talk of a duel involving the best of eleven sets. It soon appeared that their plans contained many flaws. We kept hearing different things. First we were to play the best of nine sets, then the best of 21 legs... We were being given the run-around. I was just brainwashed. In the end it came down to an hour of play, which was absolutely ridiculous. Sky Sports didn't want to broadcast more than hour but this meant that I wouldn't have the opportunity to recover if I were to fall behind. It's not possible when you're playing against the clock. I would have preferred to have played eleven sets. My management agreed reluctantly however, because we would have lost out on the 40,000 pounds if we hadn't. Chiel van Praag and Ad said: 'Eventually you'll have at least 40,000 pounds on your account and that's what you're doing it for. Don't forget that.' What they hadn't take on board, was the mental impact that losing would have on me.

At the same time, the BDO threatened to exclude me from participating in the 2000 Embassy, because they didn't want me to play against a PDC player. In addition, everyone was telling me that I wasn't going to win anyway, because Phil was better than me. That affected me enormously, even though I had two world titles to my name. I had a lot of nonsense coming at me from all sides and my broken ankle meant that I couldn't train very much. So I suffered a resounding defeat. There was also far too much of a PDC 'atmosphere' in the Wembley Arena: the referees, the stage and the PDC players who filled the hall. It all struck me as odd and no one bothered about me. All the attention was focused on Phil. If we commented on things, or when Ad, the people from SBS6 or I requested something, it was never acted upon.

The tension was terrible during the first four or five legs of the tournament. Phil was just as tense as me but he played some beautiful finishes during the next stage and things started to go very well for him. After he had won 13 legs, I was trailing way behind and there were only fifteen more minutes left to play. There was no way I could've recovered and I was no longer able to concentrate. It was over and I didn't want to participate anymore. The last fifteen minutes seemed to last forever."

Following his defeat, The Netherlands got to know Barney's other side: that of a very upset, defeated sportsman. It sent him reeling. He spoke negatively about himself on television and made an even bigger mistake by throwing a Dutch flag that had just been thrown at him, back into the crowd. This was met by a chorus of boos.

"I'd said beforehand that I didn't want to participate in this competition. I wasn't ready for it. The fear that this duel would have a negative effect on my career proved to be well founded. For me my defeat meant: 'I'm not the best.' I had let myself down and my country. The competition against Taylor came at the wrong time, in the wrong place and against the wrong opponent. I was immediately sorry about the flag incident. Someone threw the Dutch flag at me. I caught it and threw it back. Then I heard the first boo and I felt like such a failure. I wasn't worthy of the flag. 'See, you're really not capable of anything', kept raging through my mind. The inferiority complex of my younger days reared its head. The flag incident affected me most. How could I have done that?

There were a lot of people waiting for me when I arrived back at Schiphol. But I refused to look at them, choosing instead to stare straight ahead. I wanted to die. I wanted everything to die! I didn't want to live anymore and I struggled with that mental blow for two years. Only then, did the drive to win return."

"The competition against Phil Taylor was a different story", remembers **Ad Schoofs**. "Everything went wrong. Not from the outset however, as we'd sat and carefully contemplated the competition request. Obviously, the first thing we were worried about was that we didn't break any rules. A dispute in 1994 between the BDO and PDC lead to the passing of a Tomlin Order, in which the court laid down the actions and events that were permitted between the BDO and the PDC. A head-to-head was allowed, so we could pursue it further and see whether agreements could be made. We did wonder about the effect that playing such a match would have, nonetheless. The BDO was not happy of course, but there were 100,000 pounds to be divided. You can't just forget about an amount like that, so why wouldn't you play?

Reasons against playing the match arose afterwards, but these resulted only from the benefit of hindsight. The PDC played quite a game. The fact that they hadn't arranged a room for me was just one of countless examples of what felt like a cold war that was being staged against us, in order to throw Raymond off balance.

The PDC had decided that Van Barneveld would lose and that their Phil Taylor would be triumphant. Even the idea of him losing was unbearable for them. I can only guess what would have happened if Taylor had been the one to lose. Everyone who knew Raymond was aware that he wasn't able to prepare himself for the game with so much unrest around him. Things got so bad that Raymond no longer wanted to participate. I also had doubts, but in the end the competition went ahead. We just went to collect the 40,000 pounds. It was a lot of money. I told Raymond that he had to bear in mind that he might lose but he wasn't able to. He was too much of a sportsman. He told me that he had considered it, but that his heart was telling him otherwise. He was therefore extremely unhappy with the result, especially as it was disastrous and humiliating.

In the end, the competition cost him a lot and dealt a lasting blow. Throwing the Dutch flag back at the crowd had unleashed something in his mind, causing something to snap. He was no longer himself. The word 'unstable 'perhaps get close to describing it."

It all got much worse. Two months after his defeat against Taylor, Raymond was eliminated by Chris Mason in the first round of *The Embassy*. Never had he been received with so much hostility in the BDO camp as in January 2000. There was even a price on his head. Barney could no longer cope. He buckled under all the hostility and harsh criticism, and to the astonishment of millions of television viewers, severely criticised himself.

"I lost everything in the first two weeks following my defeat against Taylor. I'd lost all my confidence and it seemed as though things would never be right again. A gathering had been organised for the English BDO players on the first day of the 2000 Embassy. The person who could potentially knock me out of the tournament received a large bottle of champagne. That's how bad things had become! I played against Mason and didn't make it. Everything that had happened in the previous few months kept going through my mind. I was in pieces. If you lose, you are nothing. Nothing. Less than nothing – totally uninteresting. Only winners matter and only then are you allowed to say something. Otherwise no one takes any notice of you. This causes immense pressure. I know that I act terribly when I lose. I'm horrible and everyone has to keep away from me. My desire to win is so strong that I can't accept defeat. I just can't, whether it's a game of tic-tac-toe or a nomination for Sports Personality of the Year. If I don't win, I get really upset. 'What am I doing here?' I think to myself. It was already like that when I played games with my dad when I was younger. I couldn't stand losing, I would be awful. I don't acknowledge anybody when I lose and it takes a while for me to snap out of it.

After losing against Mason, I was inconsolable. I wanted to go straight home, so that I could feel sorry for myself and not be seen by anyone. But Ad wanted me to stay in England, so I stayed all week. I still don't know why I listened to him. 'For the fans', he said, but surely they didn't want to see a losing Barney? I always had the feeling that if I lost, The Netherlands lost too. That I'd short-changed and failed my audience. Surely if I lost, they wouldn't want to speak to me anymore or have their photograph taken with me? Some people say that a sportsman should also be a good loser. Stuff that! I can't lose. I hate it. Have a look at how John McEnroe used to react when he lost. He always looked set to kill the umpire.

A negative image of me developed in The Netherlands during that period. 'He's as happy as Larry when he wins, but if he loses, he stomps off the stage and says all sorts of negative things about himself on television'. The journalists would always say: 'Great. You're showing people that you're human. Just let it out'. But the people at home didn't understand.

My implosion in front of the SBS6 camera after being eliminated from the 2000 Embassy, had to do with the fact that I'd already been dealt a hard blow by Phil in November. Nobody understood that. I felt bad and was becoming absent minded. I was no longer Barney. It took me a long time to find my feet again after that but I had to continue. What else could I do? Go back to being a postman? Never again. I had plenty of sponsors and book-

England's moment of jubilation: Chris Mason is the great hero. He beat Raymond in the first round of the 2000 Embassy.

ings, so I could make a living just playing darts. I actually had no reason to complain business-wise, yet sports-wise I was a complete mess. Then SBS6 deserted me, choosing instead to follow Co, who reached the semi-final. The huge amount of attention that he and his wife Daniëlle received was quite rightfully earned. They deserved it. They also helped to secure adequate viewer ratings for SBS6.

I never really understood why Silvia and I suddenly ceased to exist for them though. When I made it to the final in 1999, Co and Daniëlle came to watch us make short films a couple of times. However, we weren't asked to do anything else after I was eliminated in 2000. Once again, I don't begrudge Co and Daniëlle anything. I was just annoyed by SBS6's attitude. I have discussed this with Co and we've laughed about it many times. We've admitted that there was a time both of us wished the other would be knocked out of the competition quickly, especially the European Cup, because we both wanted to be the best Dutch player. It was madness of course, because we played for the same team!

In the end, losing against Mason became the turning point in my career. A few years later, after I'd gained mental strength, the drive did indeed return. In some ways, I'm quite happy that it happened. You have to reach the very bottom to be able to rise up to the top again. If it hadn't happened, I may never have had the energy to go on and achieve as much as I did.

At a certain point a feeling swept over me, 'Wait a minute fellow, you have to go for it again. Just go and fight, because you can't go on like this.'

Losing the competition against Chris Mason also led to a period during which my opponents started to think, 'Oh, so he can be defeated.'

I faced Phil Taylor in the semi-final of the Golden Harvest in Saskatoon, Canada, six months later. I was thrashed again, losing 4-0 and two weeks later, I faced him again in the semi-final of the Swiss Open. I beat him this time and after the match, Ad and I shed a few tears backstage. Actually, that's an understatement: I cried my eyes out. It was a victory over myself more than anything. There was no television broadcast unfortunately, but I had defeated him – at the first open tournament in which players from the BDO and the PDC had faced one another. The Swiss Open therefore had the strongest field of competitors in the world. I still remember walking in and saying: 'Wow! If you win this tournament, you really are a good dart player.' I won that tournament, but the Swiss Open and the Spring Cup were my only victories in 2000."

Raymond and Co Stompé in 2000 kissing the national coach, Dennis van Onselen, after winning the Spring Cup.

Schoofs had to pull out all the stops when Raymond's career ran amiss. Schoofs remembers that terrible year: "1999 was a glorious year. Everything went well. But in 2000 things went wrong, starting at *The Embassy* and especially as a result of the television interview that Raymond gave after he had been eliminated. He called himself a 'loser'. Arjan van der Giessen, the man who interviewed him on behalf of SBS6, kept asking whether Raymond was disappointed and how he felt. He asked the same kind of question three times, which aroused a certain emotion in Raymond. Eventually, the inevitable happened: Raymond crumbled. All of the newspapers and television viewing public were talking about how Raymond had called himself a loser and a bastard. The press absolutely exhausted the story. Evidently, it is easier to write negative things about a person than positive. Are the words 'loser' and 'bastard' really that bad? Professional sportsmen and women will be able to understand these feelings completely. You have to look beyond the words. He blamed only himself. The only blunder lay in the fact that his behaviour revealed an unconscious lack of respect for his opponent Chris Mason. If he had only given him the credit to which he was entitled as the winner, his words would have been presented in a very different light. Then the opinions that resulted would probably have been completely different.

The whole of The Netherlands was disappointed. Raymond had won two years in a row and the Dutch public were waiting. Van Barneveld, who had already acquired the status of national teddy bear, would win again or at least go far. What happened after that was a pity, but you know what they say: 'What goes around comes around'. And Raymond indeed suffered the repercussions, although much too severely in effect. In the end, it formed part of a learning process.

There was another aspect to the game against Mason. The locals were completely riled, because they felt that they were losing command of their sport. They had always ruled at *The Embassy*, with the odd exception but suddenly a Dutchman had won the most important tournament in the world, twice in a row. In 1998, they thought that it was down to a spot of bad luck, but when Raymond did it again in 1999, the heartland of darts was outraged, in fact seething. It was extremely painful. The BBC was 'not amused' either. Let's be honest: it's a quintessentially English game.

In addition, the BDO wasn't at all happy that Raymond had played against Phil Taylor. They had opposed it from the start. So when an Englishman eliminated Raymond from the tournament, the celebrations could be heard in Frimley Green and across the rest of the country."

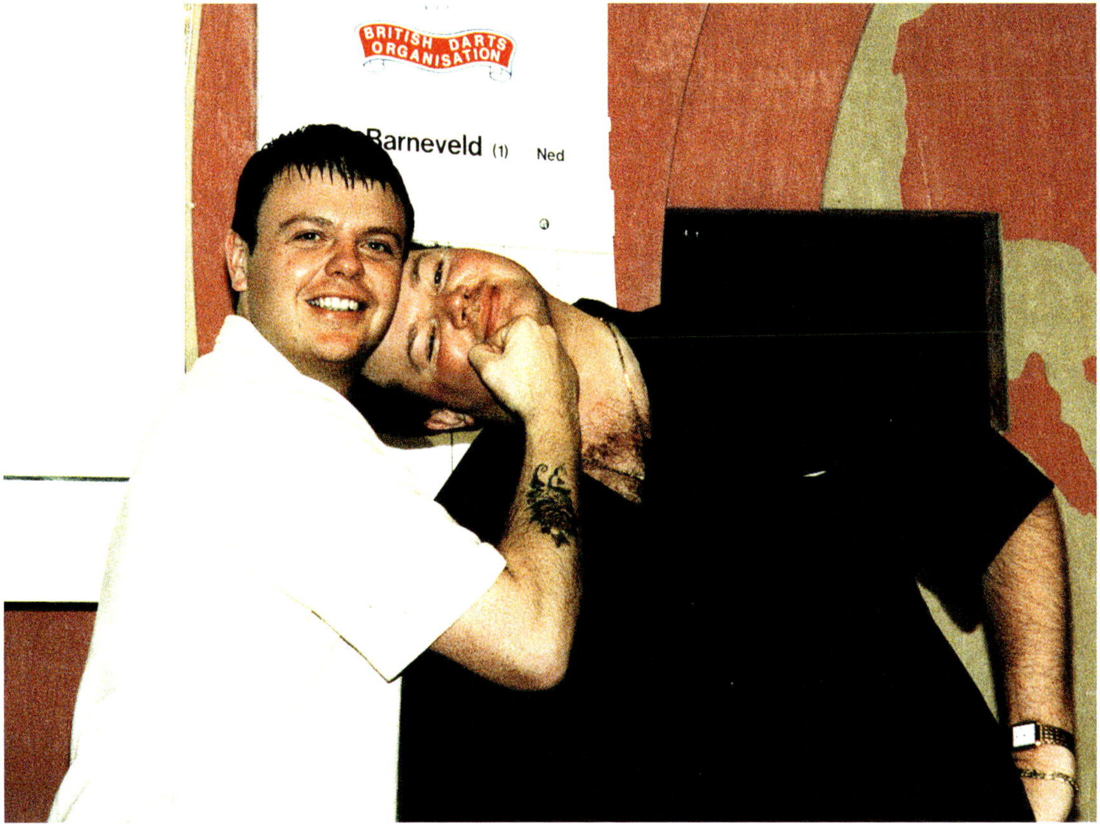

Chris Mason figurative punched Raymond knockout.

Raymond apologises to the photo of a loved one after losing to Ted Hankey during the 2001 Embassy

A heavy loss

"2001 was not a very good year either. I won the Doeland Grand Masters, the Dutch Open, the Friesland Open, the Winmau World Masters and the Spring Cup again, but I didn't make it further than the quarterfinals in The Embassy. I achieved a convincing win of 3 sets to 1 against Gary Robson in the first round, but things got tougher in the subsequent round against Steve Beaton. Nevertheless, I won that round 3-2. Ted Hankey beat me in the quarterfinal 5-4. I felt as if I'd lost another year. I'd failed yet again, to reach the top in the only televised tournament in which we were allowed to take part. The bad patch continued.

This also had repercussions at home of course. I wasn't the most amicable person to be around at that time. I kept asking myself what I was actually still doing it all for. I could participate in tournaments to improve The Netherlands' world ranking of course, but what use was that to me? Co Stompé, whose great game at *The Embassy* had earned him third place in 2000, prospered. He ranked number one in The Netherlands and was suddenly the top dog. He deserved it and he often beat me during that period. However, it made me feel as though something had been taken from me. Not by Co, but as a result of the circumstances. Co is also a much nicer guy than I am and there were plenty of people who took pleasure in repeatedly reminding me of this fact.

Dutch darting glory during the 2001 Doeland Grand Masters: Raymond, Co Stompé (middle) and Vincent van de Voort (right).

Even **Silvia van Barneveld** had difficulty supporting her husband after he had lost. "In the beginning, I would always say: 'Hey, the following tournament will be better' and 'Buckle down now'. But this only made him angrier. 'Don't you understand? I've been looking forward to this for a long time', he would say. I wanted to understand him, but I wasn't able to. In my mind there would always be another tournament. We lived comfortably anyway. Wasn't second place also a great achievement? Not for Raymond. You can listen to a professional sportsman, but you'll never be able to understand him. You never know what's going on in his head. He has to be able to cope with thousands of fans and everything else that gets thrown at him. I would like to know, but I don't think it's possible to understand a professional sportsman."

I also made the quarter-finals of The Embassy World Professional Darts Championship in 2002. This time I beat Bobby George from England 3-1 in the first round and the Belgian Erik Clarys 3-0 in the second. In high spirits, I started the game against Mervyn King, endeavouring to seal a place amongst the last four. Yet I went down against King, even harder than I had a year earlier against Hankey. It ended 5-3. Oddly enough, there followed a great year. I won the Fantastika Masters, the IDPA Masters, the Amsterdam Open, the Bollenstreek Open, The Hague Open, the Peelland Open, the Swedish Open, the Zeeland Open and the Spring Cup. It was an excellent series of wins, that I cautiously noted, confirmed that I was back on the road to success.

Raymond with the Dutch team that won the 2002 Spring Cup.

My mental dip lasted for two years, but slowly the drive to win resurfaced. Things were happening in my life that started me thinking: 'Actually, I have a wonderful life. Why am I so unhappy?'

One Sunday afternoon, somewhere in the country, I remember playing in an NDF tournament. After the tournament had finished, I gave someone a lift home. We said goodbye and he said that he had to work again the next day. This, while I would be enjoying a lie-in and doing whatever I wanted, once I had got out of bed. How lucky was that? Things like that mean a lot to me. Of the 7,000 participants in the Dutch Open, 6,975 of them had to return to work the following day."

"Don't get me wrong, Raymond was thrown to the wolves in 1998", according to **Ad Schoofs**. "And only in 2000 did he refocus. He had been living in a daze for two years. He didn't realise in 1998 and 1999 that he was still a famous Dutchman. Yet, the exalted feeling coupled with winning obviously couldn't last forever. No one can remain in top form indefinitely, not even Raymond van Barneveld. It's just not possible. I knew that he would suffer a knock somewhere along the line. It was my job to spare him from as much heartache as possible and to keep believing that he would get back on his feet again. Why else would I have continued to support him between 2001 and 2003? I knew that he would suffer a blow but also that he would recover again, if he was given the right guidance.

Raymond went through a terrible period. He was unrecognisable. He did win a couple of things during this time, but nothing made him happy. Already, under normal circumstances, Raymond is not mentally very strong, because he always doubts himself. So when someone like that suffers a mental slump, you've got double trouble. In order to improve his mental strength, you have to elevate him to an even higher level than he's ever experienced at the very top. It wasn't easy, but fortunately I had some help. Joop Alberda, who was the CEO of NOC-NSF, put Raymond in touch with Rico Schuijers, a sports psychologist from Beuningen. Raymond went to see him for mental support and guidance. I went with him on the first three occasions and listened and discussed everything. Raymond kept going there for treatment and received homework that taught him to relax. Unfortunately, the problem with Raymond van Barneveld is that if you teach him a relaxation exercise that has to be done every day, he will only do it for one day. The following day he just forgets about it. If I phoned him, he would suddenly remember, but I would have to phone him again the next day.

There's nothing wrong with this, it's just the way Raymond is. Perhaps this is why it took so long for him to recover from his slump. Every bit helps, but if you work in bits it takes longer for you to reach your goal. I spoke to him a lot and I was very firm with him. Not because I enjoyed it or got a kick out of it, but because it was necessary. I served in the military, but in all my years of service I had never met a conscript as lazy as Raymond. I simply had to guide him.

For instance, Raymond said he would go to the gym to keep fit. Or at least, that's what he said he would do. Therefore, I got him to drive from The Hague to my home in Bladel, Brabant, early the next morning. He had to be on my doorstep at eight o'clock. Obviously, he objected: 'Yes, but there are traffic jams everywhere.' I didn't care: he had to make sure that he was on time. When he arrived I took him to my gym, where I got him to train quite hard before allowing him go home again. I also travelled to The Hague to check whether he really was in the gym and if he was

Manager Ad Schoofs often had to lift Raymond's spirits during his mental and sporting crisis between 2000 and 2003. This shot was taken behind the stage of the 2001 Embassy. Raymond lost in the quarterfinal 5-4 to Ted Hankey.

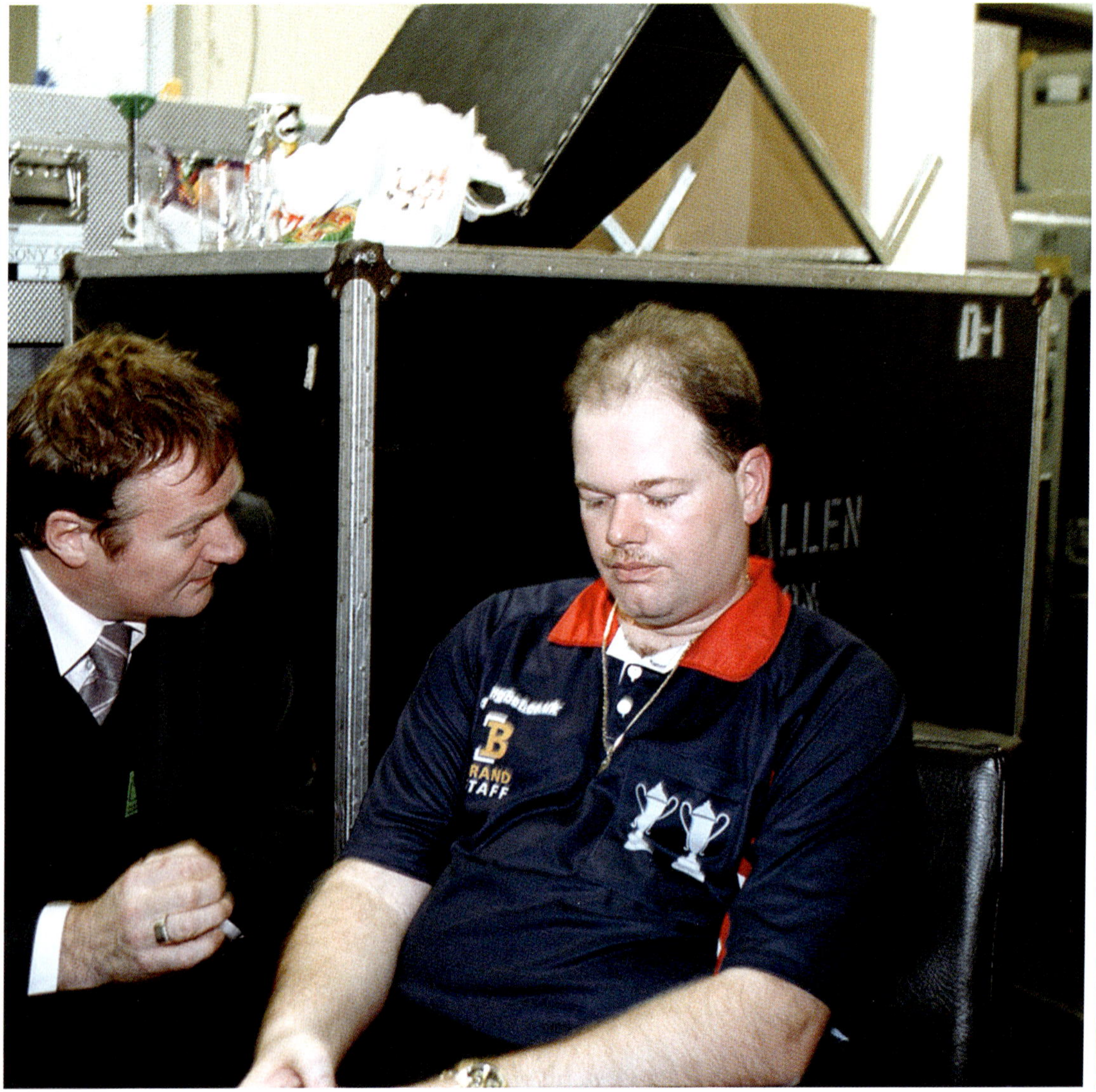

actually working out. I was not as strict with him as his father had been in his younger years. He had been even stricter. I did everything in consultation with Raymond, but I was the one that had to poke him with the proverbial stick, every day. I pushed him onwards. Raymond has no self-discipline; he can't do anything on his own. It's not in his system. He even asked me to phone him every day, because he knew very well that he wouldn't be able to do it otherwise. We were often together during this period. It wasn't always fun, but it was definitely necessary.

Raymond is congratulated by Mervyn King at the 2003 Embassy. A 5–2 victory meant that Raymond had secured a place in the final.

I saw progression and knew that eventually everything would be fine. This happened when he won the 2003 Embassy. It was a very emotional moment – for me as well. It was a breakthrough after years of investing and hard slog. As a man, you're not supposed to cry but we sat and cried together on that day. Surely that's allowed after recovering from such a deep slump? It wasn't the most emotional moment that we've shared though. Neither was the first Embassy victory in 1999, which took place under my management, nor the second round against Les Wallace (following which my wife Edna phoned me to say that I shouldn't stand crying in front of the television cameras). These were wonderful moments, but the most emotional experience for me was during a much smaller competition, the 2000 Swiss Open. I managed to get Raymond so focused that he beat Phil Taylor with an average of over 35 per dart. This was the first time that he had beaten Phil and after the match, the two of us sat on the stairs and cried. It was only the Swiss Open, but the competition meant so very much. We were getting even for the terrible competition in 1999. This victory was the first small step out of the deep slump. We both knew this and as a result, for me at least, it was the most emotional moment that we shared."

With Trina Gulliver, the best female darts player of all times, during the prize giving of the World Darts Trophy in 2003. Raymond won almost all the large BDO tournaments that year.

In 2002, the series of significant successes that led to the third successive Embassy victory in 2003 was preceded by a gruesome event. Albert Vroegop, Raymond's best friend and master caller at demonstrations, died in a fatal accident. This left a heavy mark on Raymond and placed the victories that followed in a different light.

"Ironically, my greatest successes followed Albert's sudden death. I'm still not over it and it's been a long time now. For years, I always carried a leather photo book with me when I travelled, which I used as a sort of picture frame. There were photos of my three children on one side and a photo of Albert on the other. It gave me a good feeling. Nowadays, I have a photo of him in my trophy cupboard. Albert is always looking at me, regardless of where I am in the room.

The sudden death of his friend Albert Vroegop in 2002 was a major event. Raymond and Albert were lifelong friends. Unfortunately, this friendship ended far too early.

I don't remember exactly how I got to know Albert. I think that we met in the Entertainer. What I do know is that it was in the beginning of the nineties. In 1993, he was one of a small group of people that came to meet me when I got off the boat, after my second Embassy. Albert also played darts and he spent a lot of time with Jacques Nieuwlaat, who I was also good friends with. Together with Jacques, I crossed the country to play in tournaments. At a certain point Albert also became a permanent travel companion. When he discovered that he wasn't an exceptionally talented dart player, he started specialising in what he was really good at: being funny. Albert had a fantastic sense of humour. Most people had no idea what Albert did besides play darts. He was a good friend who I could speak to about anything. He gave me lots of useful advice, especially after I had started working with Ad Schoofs. We were on the lookout for someone who could present the demonstrations and he could definitely talk a good talk. So Albert was the obvious person to be my Master Caller from the start. Ad and I also discovered quickly, that Albert always prepared well for whatever was about to happen. If we had to work at a company, he would surf the internet for days beforehand to find out information on the company. He would then incorporate this information into his text. He was always able to name at least ten of the company's strengths and weaknesses, which he did in an extremely funny way. It was also appreciated enormously. Things always look professional when you're well prepared.

We laughed and talked constantly during the many hours Ad, Albert and I spent together, driving to demonstrations and tournaments. We always played a particular game during our demonstrations, which he explained to the public beforehand. I had to throw doubles for each letter of a member of the audience's name. Albert would of course ask for the first name of the person in question. If that person then answered 'John' for example, he would immediately ask for their surname. If the answer was something like 'Baker', he would say: 'Right! Little Lord Fauntleroy!' Albert would then cover the microphone with his hand, yet making sure that everyone could hear him. The room would be filled with laughter. I would then play along, saying: 'We finally get a short first name, followed by a surname like that. Where is Pete Vis from last week? I was finished in no time with him. I only needed ten arrows.'

We once played this game at the RAI in Amsterdam. A girl with unbelievably big breasts came onto the stage. Albert asked what her name was. She answered 'Debbie', following which Albert immediately asked her if that was spelled with 'double D'. That's how sharp he was. Everyone thought it was funny, including Debbie. Knowing exactly how far to go with people, without ever crossing the line, was an art that he understood well. Another funny incident involving Albert occurred when we attended a tournament that was being played on ten dartboards, simultaneously. We presented the prizes to the ten board winners and Albert also called the worst player of the day onto the stage. He then said: 'Ladies and gentleman, this man has succeeded in scoring a total of ten points with thirty arrows. Not ten points on the dartboard, but this ten here', and he would point to the number 10 on the dartboard. He was great like that.

What I also admired about him was his sincerity. I was once asked by a good friend to play darts at his young daughter's birthday party. Her entire class had been invited to a café in The Hague. Albert, who was also his friend, had offered to come along and present everything for free, just like I was doing. That's what Albert was like. But that wasn't all. He'd also bought a birthday present for that little girl. Gestures like that are top-notch and were Albert down to a tee.

Just like the inconceivable amount of knowledge he had. When I participated in the TV programme *Weekend miljonairs*, I phoned him because I didn't know the answer to a question. It was about who had composed a particular song. He knew who had written it, sang it, performed it and so on. He knew that all four of my possible answers were connected to the song and in what way. He was spot on of course.

I was working on my PC at home in my office, when I heard the terrible news about his death. Silvia was sitting opposite me. Gerard van Dijk, a prominent figure in the Dutch darting world and good friend, phoned me to tell me that Albert had been in a fatal accident. I couldn't believe it. It hit me like a ton of bricks and I just couldn't get my head around it. As I understood it, he was riding through town on his scooter when he encountered a 70-year-old man driving his car who wanted to turn into another street. They drove towards each other and exchanged momentary glances, each expecting the other to stop. They collided and Albert was flung off his scooter. He landed, with the full force of his 200-kilo weight, on his head and died on impact. I phoned Jacques Nieuwlaat to tell him and similarly, he was completely devastated. It was terrible.

I wanted to dedicate the first World Darts Trophy in 2002 to Albert but I didn't win the tournament. Nevertheless, I dedicated my victory of the 2003 Embassy to him. It was the last thing that I could ever do for him. It's possible that events like this enabled me to put darts more into perspective, which reduced the pressure. It could also be that this led to my spate of success, but I try not to think of it too much. If I do and I happen to be sitting on the sofa at home listening to relaxing music, I tend to get very emotional. That's not good either. I try to take life as it comes, however crazy it gets."

Silvia discovered how bizarre life can seem shortly after Albert's death. It was as if their family friend was unable to say goodbye. Silvia: "Albert died not long after I had been with him to a clinic in Ridderkerk, to discuss him having a gastric balloon inserted. He was extremely concerned about his obesity and wanted to lose a lot of weight. Shortly after he died, Raymond and I were lying in bed one night, when we suddenly heard the scales in the bedroom, spinning round. I knew straightaway that it was him, I just felt it. Ever since his death, the scales at home suddenly move, giving a reading at odd times of the day. If the children happen to be walking past, they say 'Oh, there he is again.' We see this as a sign that Albert is still here. It happens in a flash and as soon as we hear it, the needle returns to its normal position."

Silvia was 15 years old when she had her first paranormal experience. "It became obvious the more time passed. It's very difficult to explain what it is, how it feels, how great it can be and also how unpleasant. Sometimes I see apparitions and other times I receive messages. It's confusing because they speak in gibberish. It's incomprehensible, but I just have to try and make sense of it. I always refer to them as visitors. Everyone has visitors around them.

It happened with increasing frequency, because I was open to it. Sometimes I didn't want it to happen, so I wondered why they still came. I know now that it was because I was searching, just like they are. They want me to help them because they know I have that gift. I don't know how to though, and that's extremely difficult. I have experienced dreadful, but also very beautiful things.

Once, while Raymond was playing darts abroad, I suddenly saw the face of my dead aunt Greet in the full moon. She was smiling. I thought that I was going crazy, but it really was her. It was so beautiful that I wanted everyone to see. I phoned my sister and asked her to go outside. She did. 'Oh my God', she said down the phone. 'I can see aunt Greet with a big smile on her face!' The way aunt Greet had made herself visible was so beautiful, as though she was saying 'I can't choose who I want to be with, so I'll just show myself to all of you.' Sometimes I sit on the sofa and I feel Albert sitting next to me. Or Michel Klooster, another of Raymond's friends who passed away. Some people think that I'm barmy. I hear: 'Why didn't you warn Albert?' But it doesn't work like that. If it did, you would be able to save the entire world. I have had to climb many mountains to be able to deal with it. I wasn't able to handle it very well, that's how difficult it is. I would always tell people when I saw things about them, without thinking how it would affect them. I confronted people with the fact that I felt a presence, and it always turned out to be true. I made a fool of myself with certain things however, blurting everything out in the hope that I would make someone happy. But it actually caused a lot of sadness for some people. That's why I no longer allow myself to be open to it."

Silvia regularly had paranormal experiences, nowadays she has no longer allowed herself to be open to them.

A proud Raymond after coming top and winning the International Darts League. The tournament premiered in 2003.

2004: A year of extremes

After his comeback at Frimley Green in 2003, an impressive series of tournament wins followed for Raymond. He rose right to the top again, winning the Doeland Grand Masters, the International Darts League, the Delft Open, The Hague Open, the Haaglanden Open, the Kempen Open, the Roosendaal Open, the Swedish Open, the Zeeland Open, the World Darts Trophy and, to top it all, the World Cup, the official world championship. Life was smiling on the former postman from The Hague.

"Sports-wise, everything was great in 2004. I may not have won *The Embassy*, which was renamed the Lakeside in 2004, or the Winmau World Masters, but I did win the International Darts League (IDL), the World Darts Trophy (WDT), the European Cup and the Doeland Grand Masters. I also won ten national and international ranking tournaments. I had prepared well for the Lakeside, which also involved training with the Australian Tony David. He won *The Embassy* in 2002 and four international tournaments in 2003, and was therefore in excellent form. My self-esteem was high as well, as I had only lost one final in 2003. It was in the quarterfinal, after having beaten Peter Hunt and Paul Hogan. I played a superb game against John Walton, which I won easily. I remember thinking, 'Who's going to beat me if I keep throwing averages like these?' My average for the entire competition was 34.61 per arrow, which I think is the highest I've ever achieved at the Lakeside Country Club. Inexplicably, however, I lost in the semi-final against Andy Fordham. To this day, I still don't know how it happened and I probably never will. I'd never even considered the fact that I could lose against Andy. I was by far the favourite to win the semi-final and all eyes were on me. The pressure from SBS6, who expected me to make the final every year, was tremendous. I don't want to use that as an excuse, but it may all have contributed to what happened. Everything went well initially and I took a massive lead, but slowly Andy managed to catch up. In the eighth set, when I was 4-3 ahead and only needed one to win, I started worrying about the pressure. Right then, with victory in sight, the chance of winning slipped through my fingers. You can't train for things like that. Our arrow averages differed by exactly 0.01 and Andy won the 2004 Lakeside. There was definitely an angel helping him out that night.

I'm normally intolerable after being defeated like that, but I think I handled it well on that occasion. I decided right there and then to go and have some fun during the International Darts League. The fact that there were now four tournaments being broadcast on television, which could earn me good money and allowed me to play in the spotlight, was very important. Things no longer depended exclusively on that one tournament in January, which always used to be the case. If you were eliminated there in the first or second round, you only pocketed a few thousand pounds. This, after a large chunk of English tax had first been deducted and your hotel bill had been paid. That had to last you a whole year. The potential income from the two tournaments organised by Ad and myself, the IDL and the WDT, created a bit more room for error though.

Raymond always relaxed in the swimming pool at the Lakeside Complex after an important competition. Here he can be seen unsuccessfully imitating a synchronised swimmer.

January 2005, Frimley Green. The coaching team has a bite to eat at "Wings on the Lake", the Chinese restaurant boat at the Lakeside Complex. Seen enjoying their meal here are haptonomist, Marco van Gorp (2nd from left), Ad Schoofs (2nd from right) and Iwe Kuitert (right).

After being eliminated from the Lakeside, I joked to my good friend Iwe Kuitert about winning the Dutch Open, the International Darts League, the World Darts Trophy, the European Cup, the Winmau World Masters and the Doeland Grand Masters. As things turned out, I lost only one competition from this entire list, the Winmau World Masters. I was no. 1 on all of the world ranking lists throughout the year, so I had nothing to complain about. Sports-wise, things couldn't get any better.

Tournament Director Schoofs (left) pays tribute to Raymond after the final of the International Darts League in 2004. Schoofs and Van Barneveld founded and owned the two large Dutch tournaments.

A number of things in my private life weren't going too well, however. Our oldest daughter, Daisy, who was 12 at the time, was going through a very difficult period. This was why I announced that I would be taking things a little easier and be spending more time with my family, during the final dinner of the International Darts League. I had been given signs that this was very necessary and, in all honesty, I also really missed being with my family. I was of course away from home for many weekends each year and often abroad during school holidays. This put quite a bit of pressure on the whole family and a girl right at the start of puberty just needs more attention. This is very normal, as is the fact that I really wanted to give her that attention.

Daisy had problems with her surname: Batelaan. It affected her life to the extent that she almost couldn't cope anymore in 2004. She wanted to take my surname, because to Daisy, I was her dad. I thought this was very sweet, as it said a lot about the bond we had. So we had her surname changed officially. I'm not her real father, but she really wanted me to be. She suffered a lot because of this and was even teased about it at school. Everyone knew that she was Raymond van Barneveld's 'daughter', but she had a different surname. Children can be very mean.

We already had a very strong bond anyway. Daisy wouldn't sleep properly all week if I was away from home, for example. But it was just impossible for me to be there all the time. I didn't have enough time to take care of her constantly. Ad Schoofs often made this very difficult for me too. For instance, I couldn't go on holiday with the family to Spain, because he wanted me to play in the Nations Cup. There was always something that he wanted me to do.

Daisy was also overweight and wore glasses. It looked like things were about to go wrong. She was pining. We took her out of her school in the newly built neighbourhood of Ypenburg in The Hague, where we had recently moved to and allowed her to return to her old school. I employed the services of a lawyer in order to get her surname legally changed. Her biological father objected, but I had cared for Daisy since she was six weeks old. We have never said anything along the lines that she wasn't allowed to visit her father. She decided for herself that she didn't want to see him.

Patty (then 10), as well as Mike (then 15), were both ill that year and at times like these you want to be there for your children. I had heard a little too often that my life revolved around darts, darts and more darts, which weren't even Silvia's sentiments, they were the children's. So at a certain point I told Ad Schoofs not to accept any more bookings for the school holidays. This was feasible but then there were other matters to be considered.

Five days away from home for the European Cup in Finland, followed by two days at home, and then five days away again for the Winmau World Masters. Goodbye school holidays. It's endless. I'm at home in between these events but I'm not the easiest person to please. I love being at home and don't really want to go away with the family when I'm not working. I'm away from home often enough.

Not long after this, his **son Mike** was injured in a bizarre accident. Mike: "I was playing darts with a friend, in Raymond's darts room at home. This guy was a poor loser. I was just writing down the score, when he threw his arrow away in a rage. It all happened very quickly and all of sudden the arrow was lodged in my left eye. I didn't know what had happened. He immediately ran downstairs, grabbed some ice and a tea towel. It gave me such a scare and I was in a lot of pain. We learned at the hospital that the arrow had penetrated my eyelid and eyeball. The tip of the arrow had just pierced my lens. If it had gone in a little further, I would have been blinded. I've been operated on three times and now have a synthetic lens. It doesn't move as naturally as a real one, which focuses and moves in sync behind the eye. A synthetic lens can't do that, which means that the sight in that eye is only 30%. If I only use my left eye, I see light and a few shadows. Sometimes it seems as though this has improved my game. With darts you have to be able to focus very well. My vision is sharper if I focus on a point using just one eye. It's ironic that it had to happen to the stepson of Raymond van Barneveld, the world darts champion."

Mike gave us a real scare. It wasn't his fault of course but it was still extraordinary that a dart had penetrated his eye this way. He came careering down the stairs but Silvia didn't believe a word of it at first, because he was inclined to play pranks. I was at the Friesland Open. When Silvia phoned me with the terrible news, she also requested that I stay there and win the tournament. They operated on Mike at the eye hospital. He'd also broken his collarbone a few weeks earlier after, falling from a motor-scooter, so he was in the wars. Silvia's parents didn't fare too well in 2004 either. My father-in-law had struggled with heart problems since 2002 and was suddenly admitted to hospital. That was a shock, because he's just a really kind man. At the end of the year my mother-in-law had to have an operation for cervical cancer. Fortunately, it had not spread. If life is going well, you tend to think that it will always be that way.

Suddenly you have to face the facts. Silvia's mother said that she was in a lot of pain after the operation but clung to the thought that the pain would eventually end. That's so brave. It really touched me. I am afraid of death – of my own and of the people close to me. Death runs as a red line right through my life. When I've built up something good, I am literally scared to death that something will happen to me. I still have a hard time coming to terms with Albert's death. We will always be linked, especially at tournaments. Maybe he could have made it big as a master of ceremonies? That was his plan. I miss him and I will still be missing him when I'm 88. Some things you can't control. I still remember when his scooter was parked in our garden. I was laughing because it was raining and he had to go home. Albert wasn't sure about riding it. He wanted to leave it there. If only he had. Knowing him, it would have taken him ages to come and collect it. He left on it though and two days later he was dead. The fact that life can end as a result of having a bad fall from a scooter, while driving at 30 kilometres an hour, scares me.

My haptonomist, Marco van Gorp thinks that I should let go of it. I remember being on an airplane, flying through turbulence when I was single, thinking nothing more than, 'Well, if it is my time to go then it's my time to go.'

Things are much different now. I have responsibilities. I wouldn't know what to do if Silvia was not here. We need each other so very much. We can't live without each other. In how many relationships can you say that? She's a great ambassador for the sport and for me personally. She joins me at many of the functions to which we are both invited. I don't know anyone who doesn't like her, even though there will always be people who take a disliking to her when they see her on television. You always get people like that. I once received a beautifully decorated letter with the words 'We Love Barney' on the envelope. Silvia opened it enthusiastically and the contents turned out to be twisted, a torrent of abuse. Silvia wouldn't let me read it. There are a lot of sick people out there.

Nevertheless, 2004 brought more than merely just misery. My father and I hadn't seen eye-to-eye for a long time, for all sorts of reasons. Fortunately, we were able to make up, which made me realise that there are always rays of hope. When I use the word 'difficult', I actually feel a bit guilty at the same time. I realise that we're much more fortunate than many other people and I'm not only referring to the heartache and pain created by terrorism, wars and flooding seen across the world. I know that I'm more fortunate than many people in The Netherlands and for that I am very grateful. Much more than I could ever express in words."

DIENST VAN HET KONINKLIJK HUIS

Van harte wens ik U geluk met het behalen van alweer Uw vierde Embassy-wereldtitel darts te Frimley Green, Verenigd Koninkrijk.

Een reeks overwinningen die getuigt van Uw geweldige klasse in deze tak van sport.

BEATRIX

Paleis Huis ten Bosch
9 januari 2005

A faxed letter of congratulations from Her Majesty Queen Beatrix.

Masters of Darts and the split with Schoofs

The reunion between father and son was good for both the Van Barneveld's. Financially Raymond was doing well. Playing in more tournaments didn't only mean earning more but also allowed less time for thoughts of doubt about himself. He continued to do well and in January 2005 won the Lakeside for the fourth time. A month later it was time for a band new tournament to burst onto the scene, The Masters of Darts. An invitation tournament in which the top BDO and PDC players could face off against each other.

"Mike had problems at school. There was an incident involving some images on his mobile phone and a girl. Unfortunately the story was completely blown up, out of all proportion in the newspapers. It was a terrible experience for Mike but also for the girl involved. It affected me a lot too. A few days after it happened, I had to face Phil Taylor in the Masters of Darts. Obviously the press was also there and I remember wondering continuously if they were going to ask me more difficult questions about Mike. It was partly because of this that I didn't feel very comfortable competing at the beginning of that tournament in Hengelo. I lost against Phil and I was also bawled out by three thousand people. That experience went straight through my soul. I had never felt that alone before. The press actually took my side and criticised the fans for their display. That made me feel a bit better. When, later in the tournament Phil beat me again, I completely lost it for a bit. The public were chanting my name and even shouted that I should go to the RTL TV studio so that they could see me. I didn't feel like doing that of course. At the outset Phil had tried to comfort me by ruffling my hair as a friendly gesture in front of the cameras. I didn't really appreciate it at the time, as it made me feel uncomfortable. Ad Schoofs and I had already put our coats on when someone from RTL persuaded me to give an interview behind the tournament stage, after all. Having done this I just wanted to leave but they thought that I should take a minute or two to speak to the fans. There would be an opportunity to do this during one of the breaks in a game that was being played at the time. Andy Fordham was in the middle of playing Roland Scholten. During this break the players remained on the stage. Unfortunately they were not told what was about to happen. Obviously, having already been banded the bad guy once, I got all the blame. Roland had a go at me. He saw it as a lack of respect for both him and Andy, playing out a game on the stage at the very same time. At a much later date Roland and I discussed this incident and cleared the air. This whole episode left a bad taste in my mouth. At the end of the day I blamed Ad for not stopping me from going up on that stage."

"Raymond had just lost against Phil Taylor for the second time in the tournament**", Ad Schoofs** remarked. "At this point Phil was already upstairs in the RTL TV studio. I wanted Raymond to be there too; But he didn't want to go. This obviously had a lot to do with the attitude of the three thousand or so people who had shouted him off the stage earlier in the week. Of course Phil didn't mean anything bad by ruffling Raymond's hair. I didn't want to push him into doing it. I pushed him sometimes but not in this case. I hoped that he would agree to an interview with RTL but he was already on his way out. Raymond didn't go to the studio in the end but granted an impromptu interview in the area behind the stage.

Raymond applauding the fans after his defeat against Phil Taylor at the Masters of Darts 2005. The drama that surrounded this tournament led to the break with his manager Ad Schoofs.

It turned out to be a negatively charged interview. The questions were mainly about being overweight and eating habits. This wasn't very appropriate, especially just after Raymond was eliminated.

Then, on the spot, Dutch RTL TV came up with another idea. This as a reaction to continued shouting by the public of 'Barney, Barney', because he had not appeared in the studio. One of the RTL producers thought it would be a good idea if Raymond said goodbye to his friends and supporters from the stage itself. Eventually Raymond agreed. I didn't get involved at this stage, so I didn't say anything. We didn't realise that their timing was rather unfortunate. RTL escorted Raymond to the side of the stage and I waited in the background. During a break in the game between Scholten and Fordham they took Raymond up onto the stage. What they obviously didn't know was that Roland, as a PDC-player, was used to remaining on the stage during the break. In order to practise a little more. Andy also stayed, even though it was not normal practice during BDO games.

The big error that RTL made was not informing these two players beforehand what was going to happen. If they had, there would not have been a problem. Raymond also assumed they had been told. Now of course Roland and Andy both thought this was very inappropriate behaviour. Everyone became extremely upset about 'Raymond's actions'. While in the meantime, the poor man wasn't aware of doing anything wrong. He just got talked into doing something he didn't want to do in the first place. I was also blamed, even though I had nothing to do with it at all.

I didn't agree with it and Raymond had only agreed in good faith. He had no idea it would turn into such an issue. Everything happened very fast. They ushered him onto the stage and put a mic in his hand before you could say 'Jack Robinson'. Then everyone came down on him like a ton of bricks. This must have been terrible for him. First he was knocked out and then they all had a go at him.

When we arrived back at the hotel Raymond watched the television interview that Roland gave after his game. It was a crying shame! He pointed a finger at Raymond as the culprit but he couldn't have known then, that Raymond didn't see it coming either. After watching this Raymond became very upset, especially with me. He said that I should have stopped him. I should have prevented it happening. However, you see, the RTL people had not asked me, but him directly instead. No matter how you look at this episode, it was not good. This also seemed to trigger the start of the break between us."

The fact that Ad had not managed to prevent Raymond from going up on to the stage became the tipping point between, as seen by the outside world, an inseparable duo. It turned out however that there was more friction, stemming from the two tournaments

"Ad taught me a lot. For example: dart-throwing demos. I am a bit of a perfectionist and I am a stickler for time. If I start at eight o' clock, I mean eight o' clock. Finishing is the same. If I'm booked for two hours? Say up to ten o'clock, then I'll stay until 10 o'clock and not later. At the beginning, when I first did demonstrations we would arrive some place or other and the people would ask if we could start a half an hour later. Fine, but I still wanted to close shop at ten o'clock. As per the arrangement we had made in the first place. 'No', Ad would say. 'Raymond, we will have to stay a half hour longer as well.' I disliked that. Ad would then add 'And what are you going to do when you get home then?' 'Well just relax, watch TV etc.' According to Ad, these kind of things were all par for the course. He saw me as an artist. So things couldn't always be expected to go exactly as planned.

These were the kind of things that I had to learn and little by little I did. In retrospect, I think that working with Ad was the best thing that ever happened to me in the whole of my career. He taught me to think ahead and not to look back. Not to dwell on the past. He always picked me up and dusted me off. He could also be extremely tough. Think about it: he served with the Dutch military for 26 years as an adjutant in the army, so he always instinctively knew how to go about things. If I felt down he used to ease up a bit but after a while he would be there again, to help me get back on my feet, to build my career.

The disastrous Masters of Darts from 2005, when the players were driven to the stage in golf carts like pop stars. Raymond had a glass of beer poured over him. He didn't seem to be able to do anything right in the eyes of the fans. On the way to the stage Phil Taylor was even hit in the face.

According to Raymond, the emergence of the World Darts Trophy and the International Darts League was the reason, indirectly, for the break with Schoofs. It was always his dream to stage a large tournament in The Netherlands. Together with Schoofs he realised his dream.

Schoofs remarked: "The Hague World Top Darts-tournament took place in 1999 at the Darling Market, Rijswijk. A year later, in a marquee on The Hague's Spui, The Haaglanden Top 16 was held. These two tournaments being held in The Hague got Raymond and I thinking. Wouldn't it be a good idea to organise a large tournament, like *The Embassy*, in The Netherlands? Actually, we had felt this might be achievable since the Brandstaff Masters was held in 1999. Back in those days, we always thought that we could never manage to organise such a large tournament by ourselves. It did however always remain a regular topic of conversation. After I mentioned it to the Dutch TV station SBS6 they immediately showed interest and we started getting things together in preparation. During the 2002 Lakeside, in a press conference, I introduced the darting world to the World Darts Trophy. Complete with a competition date and the location. A week before the start of the Lakeside I had looked over the Vechtsebanen, an Ice Rink and recreation complex in Utrecht and I immediately signed a rental declaration of intent.

When I announced the tournament we didn't have a sponsor or a TV station either to support or cover the event. We had nothing, except optimism and guts. Directly after the Lakeside Embassy we met up with SBS6, came to an agreement and started organising the tournament. We made a lot of mistakes along the way but that is always part of a learning process and to be expected. We eventually managed to break even on the venture, neither making a profit or loss. So that was good enough for us.

A year later Bavaria, the Dutch brewery, coupled up with the tournament as our sponsor. As a consequence we were able to make a small profit that year. They carried on after that and remained our main sponsor for four years. In 2003 we started the International Darts League. We went to SBS6 with this new plan just after Raymond had won the Lakeside Embassy again. The timing was perfect. They were full of enthusiasm and agreed on the spot. We only disclosed years later that Raymond was a co-owner of the tournament. It seemed advisable at the time. In order that competing players would not hold any false suspicions about how the draw was run. Which I must say was always held in public and also broadcast on television. Raymond was just a co-owner. Right up to the end of our business relationship. Now I own both tournaments."

Raymond sharing a beer with the English darts captain Martin Adams, against whom he fought many duels. As occurred during the final of The Hague World Top Darts in 2000. The duo became the best of friends through the years. After the break from Schoofs the relationship with Adams also cooled off a bit.

Ad started spending more and more time arranging these two tournaments and less time on my career. Suddenly I was no longer his core business. The World Darts Trophy and the International Darts League became his babies. In the beginning substantial investment was desperately needed but he couldn't find any sponsors willing to come up with the amounts needed. That was a pity; I still think to this day, it's great that we hold these kinds of dart tournaments in The Netherlands. The day-to-day management of them took up a lot of his time, causing him to spend less and less time to go with me to my dart demos. I did these in conjunction with Iwe Kuitert and master of ceremonies Menno Both. Later, my current manager Ed van der Veer also joined us. This all went along fine but I noticed that Ad and I started drifting apart, going our own separate ways more and more.

When organising the first World Darts Trophy, Ad had called on the assistance of Hans Rothengatter and Paul Kusters from P en H Events. They had previously organised a darts gala in Deventer, which went pretty well. So they seemed the right people to take over part of the organisation. Ad had a verbal agreement with them. Nothing was written down, just yet. After the tournament he didn't wish to work with Paul and Hans any more. According to Ad they had made a hash of it. I didn't notice any of this, as I was there first and foremost as a player. Behind the scenes there were indeed things going on that were not right. As a result Ad didn't want to do business with them anymore. Paul and Hans then started court proceedings against us and had our joint bank account and also Ad's personal bank account frozen, as a consequence. He was about to buy a new house and all of a sudden he was unable to do so. We all made an appointment together with our attorney, in Eindhoven. Paul and Hans seemed to lead us on, they didn't even show up. Two weeks later however we met. After talking things over for a while, they came up with a proposal. They were already busy arranging a tournament themselves and had reached an agreement with a TV broadcaster. It was to be a mixed PDC and BDO tournament, the Masters of Darts. They wanted to know how we felt about joining in. According to Ad it was not a problem that RTL were the broadcaster, so I signed a contract for three years.

During the 2005 Lakeside the sport supervisor of SBS6, Lex Muller, found out about the Masters of Darts deal. Then the bomb exploded. I wondered why? I didn't have a contract with SBS6, so I couldn't understand the problem. He just didn't want me to appear on RTL. I had always been available to appear in front of the SBS6 cameras but purely on a voluntary basis. Ad mentioned that if SBS6 felt like that, they should have broadcasted the tournament themselves. SBS6 apparently wanted to do that and also claimed that the sport of darts was theirs. That's when the whole question of whether I should be playing or not came to a head. As I had already signed a contract for the Masters of Darts, I was obliged to participate. A judge confirmed that this was the case, just a week before the tournament. Personally I had had enough! All this caused further problems with Ad and I was also defeated by Phil Taylor. The public turned against me and I lost in the semi-final once again to Phil.

Edwin Beijersbergen, a good friend of mine who is a bank manager with Fortis, came along to Hengelo every day to watch my matches. When all of this was over he asked me if I would be home the following Tuesday. He wanted to come round, have a chat and explain to me something he had in mind. He didn't think that Ad handled people very well and so thought he was not an asset to my career anymore. Edwin went even further, saying that if things didn't change, staying with Ad could mean the demise of my darts career. At that time I was having the same kind of thoughts. I seemed to have no more say in anything. I even felt that I should ask permission to pee. It was becoming a great burden having to report everything to Ad. I decided to step back, relax a bit and think things through. I started asking myself what I should do from now on for the best. Ronald Mallée, who used to be a manager at Fortis, now worked for the accounting firm Ernst & Young. He also had some queries concerning Ad and his work procedures. So with the aid of Ronald and Edwin I proceeded to face the situation head on. Eventually we didn't get out of it too badly, I think. The break with Ad cost me tens of thousands of euros in lawyer's costs, as well as losing my interests in both tournaments staged in The Netherlands. On the upside, the percentage of any prize money and bookings that used to go to him now stayed in my pocket.

I know that it must have been a terrible shock to Ad when the letter from my lawyer arrived one day, out of the blue at his address. Looking back, I think that I wouldn't do it like that again, if it were now. In my defence though I must say that during this period I had become an emotional wreck and that I was not able to oppose Ad personally. If I had phoned him and spoken about the situation, I wouldn't have stood a chance. I know that he would have just kept talking to me until I had changed my mind. I had to do it this way but I'm definitely not proud of it."

The first thought that crossed van **Schoof's** mind, after he received the letter from Raymond's attorney on Tuesday 22nd February 2005, was one of disbelief. "I could not believe he was doing this. Not after everything I had done for him and after all we had achieved together. One thing I knew for sure: This wasn't his idea. For a whole week after this event I wasn't able to reach Raymond by telephone. I had no idea what was going on.

It was only afterwards that I realised I had made one big mistake. In the letter from Raymond's attorney it stated that I was not allowed to make contact with him or Silvia. My lawyer advised me that it would be better if I did not contact them, because I could then be held accountable for this action in court. Looking back, it would have been better if I had just jumped into my car and gone there. Away with that! At least I would have known what had gone wrong and it could have been an honest head to head. If that had happened things might have turned out very differently. So be it. In the end it all took a long time, costing a whole stack of money and energy."

As with Raymond, the wounds caused by the break have now healed for Schoofs. "I am convinced we would still be partners if I had kept by his side, kept on going to every demonstration and every tournament with him. We had an excellent business relationship but in the end we just grew apart. It's the same as with a marriage; you should not stay away from home for too long, as that can lead to a point of no return if you're not careful. Towards the end I only saw him play at the big tournaments. It was then that our friendship started to wane, because Raymond always likes having people and support around him.

After the break Raymond said in an interview that he was mentored by me for seven years and that now he was finally able to do everything himself. I see this as a compliment. I think the best I have ever achieved with Raymond, as a person was, that I was able to point him towards having a different outlook on life. He still can't handle being beaten, which is a fine characteristic for a professional sportsman to carry. Nowadays though, he behaves with dignity regarding the press and refrains from processing his defeats until he is on his own. This is great progress. He is also mentally much stronger now. This I regard more as another achievement of mine, rather than of the procession of so-called sport psychologists that passed his door. I was the only one who always spoke supportively to Raymond before competitions. In a way I did similar stuff that a sport psychologist might attempt but more in an informal manner. I just coached Raymond whichever way he needed, to suit each occasion. We did bond. Together we shared tears of happiness but also tears of sorrow. We laughed a lot but also worried about things. This was all done to help him return to the top again and stay there as long as possible.

I think in the end I cared too much for him really. You see, if you go through so much together with some one: share each other's fears and feelings, quibble but still stick together through thick and thin, a real bond forms that eventually becomes virtually indestructible. We are like natural brothers, blood brothers. This also applies, to a certain extent, to the tie my wife Edna has with Raymond and his wife Silvia. When Silvia was not allowed to go to the 2007 Lakeside, she came over to our house and spent a couple of days with Edna. I sent a text to Raymond prior to every big competition wishing him success and also after every tournament to ask him how it went. I don't have many regrets about the things I did when we worked together. The only thing I regret sometimes is, that I didn't manage to remove some people who were hovering around Raymond who were not good for him. I should have been a bit stricter about this. Especially after 2003 there was, almost instantly, a gathering of 'guiding lights' appearing out of the wood work. Everyone wanted to share the credits then. But hardly any of them were around during the difficult years. He was criticised a lot then, often by these same people."

In 2005 the "Suske and Wiske" book "The Formidable Fantasist" was published with Raymond playing a role in it.

On to the PDC

Schoofs had always been fiercely opposed to a possible switch to the PDC for Raymond. The break between him and Raymond now allowed this door to be eased open to look through. As the 2005 darting year rolled out, the rumours of a changeover increased dramatically.

Raymond van Barneveld had by then become so much of a household name, that within the story line of the new Suske and Wiske cartoon album 'The Formidable Fantasist' published that year, there was even a cameo role for Raymond.

"The break between Ad and I was the first step. I became a free agent again and could do as I pleased. During the Masters of Darts I sat next to Steve Mottershead, Phil Taylor's manager and we chatted for a while. He told me about the ambitious future plans regarding the development of the PDC. This struck me as a very attractive venture. He also spoke about the possibility of arranging tournaments in the US, a country that really fascinates me. In comparison: the BDO only had the Lakeside, the IDL and the WDT tournaments.

With Ad in attendance, a changeover of this type and magnitude was something that wouldn't even have been discussed. He was fearful that anything like this would harm the prestige of the two big tournaments that we were involved and had invested in. This was true if I switched sides, so to speak, I would no longer be allowed to play in these two tournaments. But yes, Phil Taylor, the darting legend, was already with the PDC. And that made me cast my mind back to my youth again. I have always wanted to be the best at anything I do. Now, no matter how often I would win the Lakeside, people would always remark: 'Yes, but Taylor is not competing there.'

Eventually an exclusive contract with SBS6 became the basis of my changeover to the PDC. I had signed that agreement for one year. It gave them the exclusive rights to my availability for videos, analysis and so on. I was doing this stuff already but never got anything in return before."

Reporter Arjan van der Giessen and cameraman Paul Oberink have been following Barney around on behalf of SBS6 since 1998. Here they are in Barcelona, where Raymond is having a chat with Frank de Boer, one of the famous Dutch footballing twins.

Things sped up when RTL started broadcasting the Doeland Grand Masters in Egmond an Zee. This inspired move by RTL compelled SBS6 to also step up a gear. By signing an exclusive contract with Co Stompé and Raymond they effectively knocked the wind out of the sails of their greatest rival.

Co Stompé showing that he too has a lucky keepsake hanging round his neck.

"RTL wanted to sign me up for some incredible figure, an amount that was difficult not to consider very seriously. I didn't have to do anything in return for it either. The contract involved me being exclusively available for them to call on when broadcasting. They didn't own any rights to the large tournaments but were now very interested in buying them. They had already started with the Masters of Darts tournament and the WC operated by the PDC. RTL did stipulate with their offer that it would entail having to change over to the PDC. I decided that I would consider their offer. I did however want to speak to SBS6 first before doing so, primarily because I had a decent working relationship with them going back several years. With this in mind, it didn't seem a good idea to change over to someone else on the spur of the moment, even though the offer was incredible. SBS6's Manager of Sport Lex Muller asked: 'How much do you want?' When I told them they almost collapsed. But in the end they were prepared to pay, whatever the cost. They desperately wanted to keep me on their books. So they counter offered me the same! An astronomical amount for the sport. In addition I was able to sign a good contract with Sport1. They broadcast, among other events, the Premier League games and various other large tournaments arranged by the PDC.

I don't think that I sold my soul to secure this new contact. As, if another heavy weight TV station had suddenly implemented a tournament, with a million euros in prize money, I couldn't contractually participate. That's how it works. Regarding my change over to the PDC, SBS6 were not too bothered. Many people thought SBS6 had forced me into the move but I made the decision to change over myself. I will explain why. Primarily, as I mentioned before, I wanted to assess my actual progress, shoulder to shoulder, with that of Taylor's. I hadn't been able to play against him enough. I think however that the best players in the world can only be found at the PDC. Taylor himself stands head and shoulders above the rest.

To add to this situation, I noticed in the middle of 2005, that something was going on with regard to dart coverage at SBS6. They wanted to have the best dart players in the world competing in their tournaments. So there were meetings involving Schoofs, Co Stompé and the SBS6 top hierarchy. I wasn't in agreement with this idea. If I stayed with the BDO, players from the PDC could join in our tournaments and be able to steal 'our' prize money. Say you ended up having to play Taylor in the first round, then you were already out. I thought this move was absolutely unacceptable. In answer to these proposals I said: 'If things develop this way I am crossing over.' That in turn created another problem. As I really wanted to continue playing in these tournaments. So Lex Muller said to me: 'If you change over we will make up a plan that allows you to still take part in the tournaments. During the Lakeside tournament we could still use you as an analyst.' For me this idea was the breaking point.

The BDO didn't appreciate this very much. To them it felt like a stab in the back. I didn't really understand that. They always seemed very happy when I was eliminated from a tournament. Martin Atkins once had a hero's applause during the World Darts Trophy, after he had managed to eliminate me. I thought they would be happy that I was leaving. But no, that was also not a good idea. Naturally I understood that, for example, the English captain Martin Adams was furious with me. He is against the PDC on principle. He has said: 'I will not go over to them, not even for a million.' Well, to that message I reply: 'I still have to pay my mortgage, bye.' Somewhere along the line Adams might also be thinking that he is better placed to stay where he is. You could argue that one of the main reasons he won the 2007 Lakeside was that I had moved on? That's how it works too. Adams was very angry because he didn't know the exact story behind my changeover. He was obviously influenced a lot by Martin Fitzmaurice. The man being an expert at cajoling English players."

The important master of ceremonies Martin Fitzmaurice is famous for his unique darts call of "*one hundred and eighty*", piped out through the microphone. Not to mention being the face of the Lakeside. He links sessions, as would a successful stand-up comedian. Behind the scenes though he is often criticised because of his behaviour. "The man with the two faces" being one of his less flattering nicknames. Down through the years Van Barneveld has been a regular target for Fitzmaurice's intrigues.

"The man has never really done anything of a positive nature for me. In general he will have nothing to do with us. He thinks we are only takers. He will not hesitate to drop negative comments about the Dutch players. Also that SBS6 does not do the sport credit and that the tournaments run by Schoofs need better organising. That is, except if there was any benefit to be gained. Then he may well come over with a smile on his face and a greeting. Everything would be okay then.

Martin Fitzmaurice the BDO master of ceremonies plays an intriguing roll behind the scenes regarding his take on the Dutch.

The first time I discovered that the man was not quite what he seemed, was during the Fun&Sun Darts week in Spain. It was there that I really got to know him. During the closing evening I played a demo with Andy Fordham. I predicted how Fitzmaurice would behave and it turned out exactly as I had said. I suspected that he would verbally support Fordham during this five-legged demo. While he would probably only call out the scores for me. No extra touches like: 'Go down on your knees Barney' or 'Throw with your left hand'. These sort of one-liners appeal to the crowd. It is the swaying power of the master of ceremonies.

During the Dutch Open in 2006 there was an enormous row. Some BDO players refused to play against the PDC players. Take note, it was an 'open' tournament in which PDC players had taken part for many years. In this case he managed to influence Mervyn King amongst others, who would later crossover to the PDC himself!

In 2000, during a tournament in The Hague's Spui, Fitzmaurice even publically accused me of cocaine use. Before a tournament I often have to go to the toilet. This is just competition nerves. So the English one day decided to say that I was using cocaine. That story developed a life of its own. Now believe me, I have never even smoked a cigarette, let alone a joint. Several English players complained about Fitzmaurice and went to Rob Dingshoff. A drugs test was then required from me. I said at once: 'Great, I will go first and then everyone else can have one.' Now, you should have seen how quickly the English then revoked their request. That says enough, I think. Still, for years I carried that stamp. Even Vincent van der Voort* was told about this at the 2007 Lakeside by an Englishman. He said he knew that I was a user and that he also knew who my supplier was and where he could be found. Unbelievable. That is why I am so glad I took a drugs and doping test at the PDC-WC after my victory. I passed it with flying colours. I asked the PDC to make the result public but they did not want to. Only if a player is tested positive it is mandatory for a report to be made public. Otherwise they don't. Think about what they are saying. I play in many tournaments and finals. Then I should always be using cocaine. I would obviously not go to England by air every time, but by car? No, I hide the drugs in my hand luggage, that's a joke. And what about when I'm in America? I simply can't stand unjust stories.

But yes, Fitzmaurice seized every opportunity to make me look bad. The man is hateful, maybe because he is paid much less than the dart players. Maybe this is his way to deal with that. His jealousy has an enormously negative influence. Once again, except if there was something to be gained from it. Tommy Two face, I always call him, like in the Batman-films."

* Footnote from the writers: Vincent van der Voort is a darts player from Purmerend in The Netherlands. The two metre tall Van der Voort won his first international tournament (The Danish Open) in 2002 and has appeared regularly at the Lakeside. He managed to get to the final of the UK Open just five months after his change over to the PDC in January 2007, which is a formidable achievement.

Raymond has had some discussions with the popular dart player Andy Fordham over the years. So when Fordham, nicknamed "The Viking", won the Lakeside in 2004, he refused the lucrative change over to the PDC, partly because of Raymond's advice.

The public's number 1 favourite – Andy Fordham.

"When I mentioned to Andy in 2004 that I would never cross over to the PDC, it was because I was under contract with Ad Schoofs. If I had changed over, our tournaments would have fallen apart. So I told Andy I was staying and it was because I would ruin myself if I switched. Andy could have earned quite a substantial amount by joining the PDC but decided to remain with the BDO (also partly on the recommendation of his wife). So eventually two years later when I did change over, he probably thought something like: 'Now he is running off to make the sort of money that I could have made.' I never received a single euro from the PDC manager Barry Hearn for making the changeover. I did however receive the guarantee that I could automatically take part in the Premier League of Darts and in the WC but I was too proud to accept automatic entry into the latter. So I qualified directly for the WC on merit. I had finally placed myself in contention for the WC, a dream achievement. Within one year, coming from nowhere, I managed to reach 32nd in their rankings. That was fortunate for me but achieved on the back of another's misfortune: The Belgian Erik Clarys fell off a ladder and broke his arm in several places. This meant of course that he could no longer compete. Therefore I moved up another place, reaching 32nd in the rankings, at the last moment.

When playing at the Scottish Open I heard from various players, that Fordham was not very happy with me. During an earlier tournament in The Hague, I had played against him. I was 0-3 down but turned it around and won in the end 4 sets to 3, qualifying for the following round. All this in my home city, just in front of the Town Hall. Naturally I was extremely happy. After the winning arrow had been thrown I turned and cheered to the fans, celebrating with them. At that point Fordham was waiting to shake my hand, just for a few seconds, with his hand outstretched. Yes, a few moments passed in celebration. Then, when I wanted to shake his hand, he had already left the stage. Who was to blame? Many of the players had issues about my performances and wins from the outset. Maybe because I did well and earned a bit of money from what was in essence 'their' game. They couldn't believe that darts had become so much of an attraction in The Netherlands and that I was able to make a decent living from it. In England at the time there was not a lot of money to be made from darts. The most difficult part was that the English players from the BDO acted very friendly and nice to me. But there was an undercurrent, as with any sport played with money and big prizes involved. Strange stories did the rounds. Steve Beaton's manager came up to me once with some advice. He said: 'Raymond, you should tuck your Barney chain inside your shirt a bit more. There are a few players who think it brings you a lot of luck, so they are keen to get hold of it and throw it away.'

A month after Andy Fordham won the 2004 Lakeside, we were supposed to play together in the doubles tournament at the Dutch Open. A day before the start of the tournament he cancelled, he was sick. I was fed up. SBS6 tried to push the Dutch Darts Federation into selecting someone else to play alongside me but according to the regulations that was not allowed. Luckily I found another partner in James Wade. We even made it to the semi final together. Then guess what happened, to my astonishment? I was sitting in the VIP area and all the English players were watching the snooker, as an important final was in progress. Then during a break in the snooker match, I suddenly saw Andy Fordham entering the hall with his Lakeside-trophy. He was given an accolade immediately. This upset me and on top of that I was laughed at by several players. Why couldn't he have just told me the truth? After all I helped him a few times in The Netherlands. Several times, for some reason or other, he has not been able to show for a demo. I often had to save the day by doing it myself. But when the public expects Fordham and they get Van Barneveld instead, there will always be people who are disappointed. It's because he is a character in his own right, obviously extremely popular. Unfortunately, there were often things that created a bit of friction between us. He was once a guest on a television show in The Netherlands presented by Paul de Leeuw. He didn't get a glass of beer when he appeared, no, he got an entire barrel. In an interview he said: 'Me, train? No thanks, I'd rather drink sixty beers a day.' I didn't appreciate that. This could harm the sport. A world champion weighing in at 200 kilos; who says that he doesn't have to do anything about that? Other players on the circuit were also not very happy with this kind of remark.

Unfortunately, since the 2007 Lakeside his health has not been so good. I find this sad. I would not wish it on anyone. Possibly he thinks, that because of what I said, his dream didn't materialise but in the end he decided to stay with the BDO, himself. I didn't make this decision for him. Afterwards you question yourself 'What is this stuff all about?' It's time that we had a drink together and a bit of a laugh."

Fordham came out as winner of the Lakeside in 2004, with some good wins along the way, including a sensational victory over Raymond in the semi final. After this he turned down a very lucrative offer to go over and join the PDC. Partly on recommendation of Raymond, who in fact went himself, after his circumstances changed in 2006.

By winning the 2006 Lakeside, Raymond could have equalled the record of the legendary English dart player Eric Bristow. He had won The Embassy five times, which earned him a "royal title". Bristow went along to Frimley Green especially to meet Van Barneveld. Unfortunately Barney lost in the final against Jelle Klaasen and so remained on a total of four victories.

A glorious future

In 2006 Raymond took part in the Lakeside for the last time in his career. He made it to the final again. There, Jelle Klaasen was just too strong for him and took the title, in an extremely thrilling game. Not long after that he told the world he had crossed over to the PDC.

"All the preparations for my changeover were already made before the start of the 2006 Lakeside. The only thing that I hadn't done was sign. The eventual signing took place at the beginning of February, one week after the Dutch Open. So I could still change my mind and turn back for some time. Barry Hearn was one of the people who really wanted me to make the switch. However I did have my doubts about actually doing it. How would everyone react at the PDC? There were people there that I couldn't class as being my best friends. They were also definitely not looking forward to seeing me there. I had even clashed with some of them in the past. See, when they changed over to the PDC I was quoted in the media as saying that: 'we would miss them like having a toothache', because they had never really achieved much at the BDO. Anyway it was a truism but looking back I could have been a bit more subtle. Mardle said after his crossing: 'I am going to the 'Premiership of Darts'. I reacted in an interview by saying: 'Funny that! So that makes our league, the Championship division, where you didn't have much success. What are you expecting to gain in the Premiership?' Yes, sometimes it may be better to keep some thoughts to myself, when I speak to the press. But I did mean it.

The defeat in the Lakeside final against Klaasen was an enormous downer. I felt as if the entire Netherlands had turned against me, yet again. Jelle* was welcomed back to his hometown enthusiastically. Great! I thought but then in the background I heard the public singing 'Who the f***k is Barney?' This hit me hard. The Netherlands just didn't get it, I felt. This country, that loves its sports so much, cannot sit comfortably with its heroes.

Fortunately my switch to the PDC went well. During the early weeks after my move I was received with open arms. Also by Mardle and Jenkins. With the latter, Terry, I always laugh myself silly, everything we do is always a lot of fun. I also apologised sincerely for the things that I did wrong. Painter said to me: 'Geez Raymond, you don't have to explain anything to me. The mere fact that you've dared to make the change and by doing so give the PDC a new boost, says enough already.'

The BDO was very important to me. I owe my lifestyle and career to it. The only thing I was not happy about was that they didn't expand enough as the sport grew in popularity. If Ad and I had not been around, the two Dutch tournaments would never have materialised. What would the BDO darts players have survived on then? At the PDC they know that they are working with professionals and act accordingly. I don't know why the BDO trails behind. Maybe they need some fresh blood over there? Or maybe they have already experienced their best years and are too set in their ways? Adams and Fitzmaurice, members themselves, also have been known to complain

* Footnote from the writers: Jelle Klaasen surprised almost every darts enthusiast by winning the Lakeside in 2006. By doing so, the then 21 year old Dutchman from Brabant became the youngest Embassy/Lakeside winner ever. Klaasen, who up to then had won six Dutch tournaments, earned his place by winning the qualification tournament, which was an achievement in itself. He had a difficult year after winning the Lakeside title but is still regarded as one of the most promising players in the darts world.

about the workings of the BDO. If I had anything to say about things though, they never agreed with it. All of a sudden it seemed that any form of criticism was too much.

The worst part of it all was that Silvia was not welcome at the 2007 Lakeside. She had a difficult time during my changeover to the PDC. She saw the BDO as family and wanted to go there to see everyone. She was plainly turned down. A hotel and flight, everything was arranged, paid for and taken care of. The BDO decided that Silvia would not be allowed to attend. If she came she might attract too much attention. She was informed that if she arrived she would be removed by security. It would seem that Fitzmaurice was also involved in this. Since then I have cashed in my chips, so to speak, with the BDO.

My changeover came out as big news in England. My first game after joining the PDC was in the Premier League against Ronnie Baxter. The venue was in Blackburn, where I was incredibly well received. I won 8-1 on the night. The public chanted my name constantly, it was great. The other side of the PDC coin was also introduced to me, very quickly. The first qualifying round for the UK Open was staged at a pub in London. There was a row of four dartboards laid out in the pub. 'Oh my God, what have I gotten into?' I thought. I lost against Steve Evans from Wales in the first round. Great eh? Luckily I did manage to win the second and third qualification tournament. In the middle of all of this I threw a 9-darter in a Premier League game against Peter Manley. Later that same evening I drew 7-7 against Phil Taylor. My introduction into the legendary PDC was going tremendously well.

In England I gained the respect of the people. My English supporters follow me around. There's a so-called 'Barney Army' and they even dress from head to foot in orange. Strange, in The Netherlands I am often hissed at. But I must say that the mistakes I may have made in The Netherlands, I will not repeat in England. Defeat can become like an act in a play. Maybe a professional sportsman has to be able to act. Personally I can't do that, I didn't go to drama school. You can clearly see that I am totally pissed off when I lose. The locals understand this better than most. Apparently they have some weird affection for me. I am recognised everywhere I go in England. That starts the moment I land and step into a taxi. That is really great. Fans treat me with respect. If I am having dinner somewhere, they don't ask me 'May I take a photo, please?' But: 'Geez, we think you're great and we always see you playing well on TV. When you are finished, could we please take a photo?' That's a totally different approach than in The Netherlands. 'Can you pose for a photo?' is what they say. When I reply that I am eating and don't really want to, I am immediately branded as self-important.

I have developed a great love for England but I must admit that an English breakfast is not for me. When I arrive I will have one in the beginning but then not again for a long time. Driving on the left hand side of the road is not so difficult in general. I did once, nearly have an accident but these days I almost never drive myself. We mostly take taxis and in England this is an experience in itself. The enormous legroom you have in the back of a traditional English taxi is wonderful. There are two things that, as a Dutchman, I find uniquely English. Number one, they will gamble on everything and I mean everything and number two, they don't care how much they have to pay for an entry ticket to an event, they just pay it. There are no half-filled halls in England. People just want to be there and if you make it, then you are *The Man*. You can then tell everyone for years that you actually saw, in person, Van Barneveld and Taylor throw. You become a sort of folk hero yourself. In The Netherlands the public think that 50 euro's is too much to pay for a ticket, without even questioning what you get in return. So they stay at home. The English, on the contrary want to be there, in the middle of the action. That's a purely English take. The English also have a genuine sports culture. They grow up playing and watching sport. It's a part of their upbringing. A day-to-day family event. The English also spend more time going out than the Dutch. After I have finished a darts demo somewhere, when leaving the premises, there are always a couple of fans outside smoking. I always make sure I have a few words with them. At that moment they have no idea what's going on, because sportsmen are normally big, distant heroes in their eyes. Then, suddenly, they are face to face with one. If I ask them if they are enjoying themselves, they normally reply: 'Now? It's the best day of my life.' That says a lot. That makes me very happy.

It's just a bit of a shame, that so far, that even though I have been coming to England for a long time to play darts, I haven't had much spare time to see a bit more of it. Still, I love the country.

This wasn't the case beforehand, as I didn't know the culture first hand. There is a different mentality in England. I'm not allowed to hand out free photos of myself. That way you ruin the market, they say. If I had to ask the public to buy a photo in The Netherlands they would reply: 'Hey, are you crazy or something? Pay you for a piece of paper, get lost!' This is how the average Dutchman thinks and acts. In England if you support Arsenal, Manchester United or Liverpool, you may buy a new home and away kit every season. You do this because the club is dear to your heart. In The Netherlands they say: '60 euros for a football shirt, that's far too expensive. I'll go and buy a fake one at a jumble.'

In England they see me much more as an entertainer. After the 9-darter against Manley in Bournemouth I went out to buy a kebab. Everyone around spontaneously started singing: 'There is only one Raymond van Barneveld.' I wasn't even allowed to pay! I signed all their tickets and they walked away feeling on top of the world, proud to have met me.

When I walk the streets in The Netherlands the same does not often happen. I will be recognised and the people normally call out something like: 'Hey Barney, 180.'

What I do find a drawback in England is that everyone wants to shake your hand. I don't have nosophobia but shaking hands the whole day is really tiring. Sometimes a person wants to do it three times, when they meet you, when they say goodbye and even in the middle of the conversation!

Dutchmen are not so enthusiastic. I will never meet a lot of peoples' expectations of me I guess. I have learned that. I will not make the same mistakes in England. I don't want to spoil things for myself. Once I was training in Eindhoven, when someone actually walked up to the dart throwing line and asked for an autograph. I said: 'Not right now, I am training.' He immediately got upset and stormed out. At the end of the training session however I sat at a table with 32 people and we laughed and talked for around 2 hours or more. As I was about to leave I gave them all a Barney mouse pad. Everyone had a great evening. But the only thing you heard later was the story of the disgruntled autograph hunter. People have to understand that with those three arrows in my hand, I am lethal and everyone should stay away from me. As soon as I have put my darts away I become a totally different person."

After the game in which Taylor and Raymond drew, there followed a defeat at the hands of "The Power" in the Premier League. This happened on Raymond's birthday, 20th April, 2006. After this second loss, the wheel of fortune started changing directions though. Van Barneveld won the UK Open, his first Grand Slam while with the PDC. He defeated Taylor and repeated the act in Las Vegas.

"During the UK Open Taylor missed three check-out arrows and I threw a 97 finish using two darts. I jumped up and down on that stage like a clown possessed, that's how happy I was. It was the first time that I had ever managed to beat him in a main line tournament. Taylor didn't have a problem with me beating him. He understood. In Las Vegas, during the Dessert Classic, he missed a finish as well before I was able to end the game. The summer of 2006 was wonderful. In May and June I won the IDL, took the third place in the Premier League, won the UK Open and was runner up in Vegas. I actually missed qualifying for the World Match play through wanting to watch the Dutch football team play the Ivory Coast in the WC competition. Only after that did I start to throw. Too late, I lost 5-4 to Andy Hamilton.

From that September I started concentrating on the PDC WC. I had by then already split with my PA and coach of the time Iwe Kuitert. He was Schoofs' successor but he guided me more specifically in the sports area. This he managed extremely well. Look, he had been my friend for years and often travelled with me anyway. What could be better than giving him an official title? So I hired him, but after a while I figured that I needed someone that could also take care of the business side of things for me. Unfortunately this was not something up Iwe's street. We eventually parted company, which was quite painful for both of us. Luckily, time, coupled with a good heart to heart chat, has managed to heal all the wounds and today we are back to being the best of friends.

The idea was to do as much as possible myself but pretty quickly I discovered that this did not work. I found that I not only needed someone to coach me with the sport but also with the day-to-day business aspects of my darting career. The man who stepped into these shoes was Ed van der Veer. Ed came out of the trade and industry sector. He'd been working for me for years as a master of ceremonies so he also had the necessary knowledge of darts. I asked him in October 2006 to accompany me on my rounds and see what he thought. He came up with some excellent tips. He asked me for example who I was training with. I replied: 'With Co Stompé, Edwin Max or Vincent van der Voort.' He then asked what game length we trained with: 'Well, best of eleven, or best of thirteen sets.' No, he wanted me to play all thirteen sets. Not stopping if one reached seven, as we did normally. The reason was that he expected a final of the WC against Taylor to quite possibly go all the way. With hindsight, he was absolutely right.

During 2007 Ed continued to work for me more and more. All the tournaments at which he was present had ended really well. He also put into place similar things to what my previous managers had done, for example: Forming a business and career structure, managing training schedules and wanting me take part in other sports to keep fit. Apart from that, his input was valuable because of the way he approached marketing and the plans that he made. This made me feel good, as my business matters were now also developing more.

Ed, above all, is always prepared for what he has to do or say. He always thinks things over beforehand and I find this great. If I ask him why he thinks things should be done differently, he always comes up with a good argument to support his case. This is one of his strengths. We co-operate and agree after we have discussed the subject together. He doesn't just tell me what to do, full stop. We talk a lot and discuss everything. This method allows me to propose ideas and I also know that my side of a discussion is taken seriously. If I have a good idea Ed is open to it. This to me is an ideal formula and the main reason why Ed is now my fulltime manager.

Raymond with Iwe Kuitert, his good friend, who also managed his sports career for a short while.

In the run-up to the WC, Silvia and I, together with my parents, enjoyed a long holiday in Thailand. Just the four of us. Telephones off, it was wonderfully relaxing. When I returned I felt as good as new. I was in super shape and form.

In the first round of the WC I was drawn against Mitchell Clegg, a boy of 16 years; I won 3-0. After that I played against the No 1 seed Colin Lloyd. My form I thought was good, but before I knew it I was behind 0-3 sets. I didn't understand it. Luckily I was able to remain calm. By already going 0-3 down, nothing seemed to matter any more. A weight seemed to roll off my shoulders and I started throwing very well. I pulled up level to 3-3 and then the last set turned out to be extremely exciting. I continued the pressure but was always playing catch up with each leg. Then we were level at 5-5. In order to decide who threw first in the last leg we then threw for the bull's eye. The one who threw closest to it gained the advantage of starting first. It was me. …The last leg was mine."

Raymond steam rolled through to the final without any problems. There, waiting to meet him in the final, as if it had to be that way, was …Phil Taylor. Eleven months after his changeover Van Barneveld now had to prepare himself for the biggest competition challenge of his darting career.

Raymond and Ed van der Veer his current manager celebrating his win in the WC, at the expense of Taylor.

"There was a break during the WC, so I was able to spend a few days over Christmas with my family at home. New Years Eve was however spent in England with the SBS6 crew at a local Chinese restaurant.

2007 was just 30 minutes old but I was already in bed, because that evening it was the game against Taylor.

He began powerfully! I couldn't hit anything and quickly fell behind 0-3. He didn't give an inch. Yet, I also didn't go into panic mode once either. I was playing in a sort of trance and suddenly realised that I was ahead 6-5. I don't know where this sudden calmness came from but I'm convinced that there is more to heaven and earth than meets the eye. Someone up there thought it was my turn to win.

The final was not to be won until the end of the last and deciding leg. I started with 100, and then Taylor rolled me over with 180. That scared me a bit, but I countered with another 180. It was with his next throw that Taylor conceded the title. He could only manage 40. I answered with 105 and failed to finish on 116 but eventually won with double top.

Throughout the entire final I wasn't nervous at all. This I credit to the meditation classes I was attending, given by my Zen master Rients Ritskes. In the preamble to the WC I had learnt to meditate three times a day, for twenty minutes. This indeed relaxed me and eventually helped me win the world title. Normally my heart would beat extremely fast during a competition but not this time."

At the PDC World Championship in January 2009, Barney shook off a very average 2008 darting year in one go or rather in one throw! He beat Mark Stephenson (3-0), Wes Newton (4-1), Ronnie Baxter (4-3), Jelle Klaasen (5-1) and James Wade (6-4) to reach the final for the second time in three years.

The quarterfinal against Jelle Klaassen was especially memorable. Not only did Barney recapture his best throwing form, he also threw a 9 darter! The very first one recorded in the history of the PDC WC.

The roar of appreciation from the fans rang round a sold out Alexandria Palace as Ray's prize checkout arrows hit their target during the first leg of the final sixth set, one by one.

Triple 20, great!

Triple 19, excellent!

Then…Double 12, amazing. Result!

Unexpectedly and just the same as he did in 1998 with the BDO, Raymond wins the PDC top prize in 2007: The World Darts Champion.

The 2500 darts fans went wild with joy, they hit the roof but Raymond remained outwardly calm. He kept focussed and went on to beat Klaasen comfortably.

The 9 dart finish earned him a bonus payout of £ 20,000. However, this time in the final Phil Taylor proved too strong for Barney. The match ended 7-1 but due to his overall performance in the competition, Raymond restored his top line status.

"During the run up to the WC I started to feel better and better. I also decided to throw using my old familiar darts again. I've found that playing with them makes me feel more comfortable. Why is that? I think if standing on the stage wearing a pink sock on one foot makes a person happy, that should not be a problem. Little things like that make me feel good. I've also had two shirts especially designed for me.

I trained intensively for a week with Mervyn King in preparation for this WC. That definitely helped both of us, because Merv made it to the semi-final! I was keen to show what I could do and to perform well.

How I managed to do that was of course also partly thanks to the challenge from Ronnie Baxter. It was quite a game that third round. He threw high scores consistently and had many good finishes. In the final leg, the sudden death, at checkout he still had two arrows left to finish on double eight. I was sure I was out. Finished. I stood there really fed up, and then what happened? He missed. Twice! That had not happened during the whole game up to this point. Gratefully, I then was able to throw a double top to finish the game. It was disappointing for Ronnie but as he said afterwards 'Whoever throws the last double is the best man.'

As a result, I played Jelle in the quarterfinal. That win meant a lot to me because I lost to him in the 2006 Lakeside final and I count that as a blemish on my career. I should never have lost that duel. Maybe that was why I was throwing so

well this time. I think it was my best match of the tournament. This together with scoring the 9 darter in the same game! A dream come true. Outwardly, I remained cool and calm but inwardly a lot was going through my mind. I knew that nobody else had ever thrown a 9 darter at the WC. That made it extra special.

The response of the fans in the hall was overwhelming. In fact, it was like that during the whole tournament. The Barney Army were tremendously supportive. I'm sure that their encouraging cheering helped me through some difficult moments. The only downside was that it didn't work in the final. Yes, Phil played out of his skin. He was untouchable during this tournament. How does he do it? I don't know but he's simply the best."

MASTERS OF DARTS
Champion
Masters of Darts 2007
KEUKEN CONCURRENT
Nifra.nl
Shipbuilders
AFAB
BULLIT
ENERGY DRINK

Review

By defeating Taylor in the WC final, Raymond had reached giddy new heights with his illustrious career. In the weeks and months that followed he managed to win one title after another. The victory over Taylor worked more than just being a major release of tension. Raymond finally seemed to be at peace with himself. Was he now the best or not? That could be decided at a later date.

"By the summer of 2007 I had already eight titles to my name: The WC, Newcastle, Gibraltar, the Masters of Darts, Pro Tour Germany, UK Open, Pro Tour Las Vegas and the Las Vegas Dessert Classic. At the US Open I lost in the final and competing in the Premier League I got knocked out in the semi final. In everything that I played in I managed to go a long way.

Since his switch to the PDC Raymond is also more relaxed about the house**. Silvia**: "When Raymond has to play darts, we don't often watch it at home. Mike normally has to leave the room, because he usually starts yelling at him if he doesn't throw well. The girls don't watch that often either. It is too stressful for them. They know that if Raymond loses, he may need two days to cool off and feel better again. They understand but at the same time they also find it difficult to cope with. Since he has started playing with the PDC he has become much more relaxed though, as he wins a lot!

I can't really support him directly with his career. We can only be there for each other and trust one another. In every relationship you have to work hard to keep it strong and healthy. We also have an extra challenge, the publicity. If we do anything or something is written about us, we have to explain everything to everyone in the street, everywhere. 'It can't be true, can it?' 'No, it's not', I might have to repeat about a hundred times a day. I support Raymond with his career decisions. For example his decision to switch to the PDC. I hated it at first but now I see that he made the right decision. The way I saw it was, that it was not about money but more about the people at the BDO. I loved them. I must say though that with the PDC he does get much more respect for his work and he earns more. That's good for his peace of mind and because of that he's a much happier person nowadays.

He now finds darts more satisfying than previously and this contributes to him winning a lot more often. The only disadvantage is that he is away from home a lot now. Still, if I go to watch him play and he winks at me from the stage just before an important match, I feel our connection. Raymond is so different from me but also extremely loving. On the one side he seems like a child but on the other he's very responsibly minded. He knows much more than he thinks he does. He's clever and has good ideas. But he's still as insecure and easy to influence as ever and I can never understand this. Ray has become a businessman. He speaks and writes proper English quite well now. I admire that. But yes, don't they say: 'Every person has a weakness.' Well, with him it comes out when he loses!"

Silvia supports Raymond through thick and thin. Even when she had to say goodbye to her dear friends at the BDO.

It is difficult to say how good I am. I play with much more confidence now. I was always so stressed out before. Maybe because I could never normally play against Taylor. Also when I did, I always lost. I couldn't live with myself like that. I had to catch up with him and play the guy. I have stopped trying to analyse who is the better player. In 2006 I still allowed it to play on my mind. In May 2007 I lost against him three times. It took me a while to regain my confidence afterwards. I had to remind myself of all the titles I have won and look at all the trophies I have at home. After that I won a lot.

Now that I have found closure for certain issues, I can enjoy the rewards of what I have achieved more. I have stopped now with the Zen. I think perhaps that it relaxes me too much and that's not good either. I need adrenaline. I have to feel the tension. I think the reason I was defeated in the semi final of the Premier League was partly because of the meditation effect. I was too relaxed on the stage. 'Well, even if I don't win, it doesn't matter.' That's of course not a good mentality either.

I once saw a fortune-teller. She predicted that I would always come second. I would win sometimes but there would always be someone better than me. This seemed to be true for a long time during my career. If it wasn't Ronald Wensveen, then it was Co Stompé or Roland Scholten. You name them. I've always had stiff competition up against me. Always. I did, in the end reach the top, so this prediction proved not to be entirely correct. Just like playing against Phil Taylor. I have craved to be the better of the two of us for years. The best in the world. At a certain point, after he had beaten me over and over again, I had to admit that he was the better player. That of course, in itself is nothing to be ashamed of, because he is extremely good.

Raymond in 2007 during the PDC WC, playing against Taylor.

I grew up with 'The Power' being my hero, who by then had already won *The Embassy* twice, the Winmau World Masters and the European Cup. I have always been an extremely big fan of Phil Taylor but I didn't know him. When I was eventually able to play against him, I was overwhelmed with emotion because, there I was playing against a darting legend. That was a very strange experience.

He supposedly once said that I was the best dart player in the world but that I didn't know it yet myself. Also according to Phil I'm the only person who can make him nervous in front of a dartboard. There are some people who say that I'm better than him. I know that I still want to be the best. Whatever the truth, I can say that I have looked him in the eye and faced up to him. I also find it more important to win against him than to win any other tournament.

Phil 'The Power' Taylor, the man with more world titles than anyone else, also has his own vision of Raymond and his darting achievements. **Phil Taylor:** "Now that I have been beaten by Raymond, I'm paid more attention, than when I used to win almost everything. He has forced me to become a better player. This is good. I am still trying to improve myself, as I am still ambitious. In the upcoming years I will develop a method that will give me a perfect style. So good, that I will always be able to throw a 9-darter on television.

Everything Raymond has done in the last couple of years, he has done well. If I were him, I would stay in this mould. He has been really worried about his weight but why? Stay as you are, I say. He is a better player when he is overweight. If he tries to change, it may influence his game. When Raymond starts sweating and comes under pressure, he is at his best. I also play better when I'm overweight. I like Raymond a lot; he is a friend of mine.

His decision to join the PDC has proved to be a good one. He has to work harder now. He has become a target and a goal, very quickly, just like me. Everyone wants to beat him. He will improve because of this. I heard that his main aim, when changing over, was to be able to challenge and beat me. This in order to see just how good he could become. That's fine. It's important that you stretch yourself as much as possible in your sports career. I also want to know how much better I can become. So we are both extremely focused on trying to be the best in our field. That must be good for darts!

When I lost the world title to him in January, I could afford to relax for a whole year afterwards. I started to focus on the winning the title back. The final between Raymond and myself in 2007, was the best final ever. That's not only my opinion, but also of the fans. I've been involved in many finals, but this time it was different. When I threw 180 in the last leg, I thought I had him beaten. But Raymond fought back. He played extremely well, out of his skin! It was pure, exquisite entertainment, the hall went mad! He had already displayed his comeback talents in the second round against Colin Lloyd. Raymond is an excellent opponent. One who never gives up. Never ever."

Raymond celebrating his win over darting legend Phil Taylor in the final of the 2007 PDC World Darts Championship held at the Circus Tavern in Purfleet.

Father Rob: "I'm no Rockefeller or the like, but the children have never gone short. Everything I could possibly manage to provide through the years I have given them. When I was a child all I used to get was something small like a little car at Christmas or Sinterklaas. I promised myself I would never let that happen to my children...

Now that I have been driving the truck less these last three years, I see Raymond more often. I only drive at weekends. All through the week I am at home. Since 2006 I have lived only ten minutes down the road from where he is. It's really nice to have more time for him and see him regularly. He has bought a new office which I am going to renovate for him. I have it all planned. I really enjoy doing this for him.

When I compare him to the way he used to be I am not surprised about the way he developed. I remember vividly when we played Stratego for the first time and he got angry because he lost. He swept all the pieces off the board and I almost pulled his hair out. His character is quite similar to mine. He always wants to win and so do I.

His problem has always been that he can't handle losing. I can. If I say anything about it he says: 'But do you know how I feel when I lose?' Yes, I do know exactly. I hate losing just like him but I manage not to show it. I would always shake everyone's hand and in his case, speak to the press decently."

Mother Anneke remarks that she thinks her son is improving: "Since Raymond managed to beat Phil Taylor on 1st January 2007, I think he's changed a lot. He's not so negative about everything anymore. That makes me feel really happy. Ray has always been a kind boy, to date he has never talked me down. In 1998, when he won *The Embassy* for the first time I was in the crowd. It was the first and the last time. The most wonderful moment I thought was when he fell down on his knees and cried after throwing the winning arrow. 'That's my son, who has just pulled that off', flashed through my mind. I congratulated him in the player's lounge. I said: 'Raymond 'I'm proud of you, I'm really very proud of you.' 'Yes mom, are you really?' he asked in reply. Raymond obviously has some negative issues the same as everyone I suppose but he's really a very nice boy. In the days after the victory there were a lot of reactions to contend with. The telephone constantly kept ringing. I received a large bouquet of flowers from the manager of the supermarket where I always did my shopping. 'You may always stay in the background, but you must have done a lot for him to be able to get where he is', he said."

I now have an amazingly strong bond with my father. What happened in the past has shaped me. He is very distrustful. There are very few people that he trusts. I would say 'Why do things always have to be the way that you want?' But if something is wrong these days I phone him and only him, nobody else. It's really strange. I now experience similar moods like he used to have. I can get derailed. If I lose, my world starts imploding. I really feel it that way. That's not a healthy way of thinking of course. After I have lost I disappear into my bedroom and I won't come out again until the following day. I think this has got something to do with the fact that I used to feel I wasn't really good at anything. Until I picked up those magical three arrows, that was. Suddenly I had found my mission. This I feel is partly why I struggle so much with losing, I am failing in my purpose."

Standing in pole position with 34 wins Van Barneveld is well ahead in the BDO's victory classification, The legendary Eric Bristow follows with 26 in second place and Martin Adams, the only top classified player who is still actively playing in the BDO, stood at 4 with 16 victories in the Summer of 2007. A long way behind.

Thanks to his run of victories in 2007, when he won almost all of the large PDC-tournaments, Raymond has also discovered that Phil Taylor is not undefeatable. Now this idea has to gel in his mind and replace his lack of self-confidence, which still takes up a lot of his energy. After his successes during the 2007 darting year, when he even managed to top the Order of Merit, Raymond hit a dead point in 2008

"Up to the middle of July 2007 I had a superb year. Then I hit a bit of a dip. I was eliminated in the first round of the World Darts Trophy and in the WC I was defeated in the quarterfinals by Kevin Painter. The slum unfortunately continued into 2008. I changed arrows and other equipment quite a bit. If that doesn't work then I will search else

Rob and Anneke van Barneveld sitting at home on their couch displaying their most cherished photo of Raymond.

where to solve the problem. This is still my insecurity working against me. You never want to blame yourself do you? So I keep looking for other reasons. If I think that I will play well with a red sock on one foot and a blue one on the other then I will!

In July, during the World Match Play in Blackpool, something incredibly weird happened. I totally froze against Mardle. I was ahead 12-7 and then wham! I lost eight legs in a row. The public shouted 'Easy, easy!' It was as if their chanting went right through me. This wasn't Raymond van Barneveld any more. No one could normally take eight legs in a row from me. Then I threw the better to take the next three legs, after which I missed five finishing arrows to make it 16-15. Wayne eventually came through and won 18-16. This was my lowest point. I took a month off and seriously considered stopping with darts. I had had enough. Totally.

The "Barney" trophy is given to encourage talented sportsmen from The Hague.

The darts sabbatical lasted a month, even though some claimed it lasted two. Don't I also have the right to a holiday? The month of August was holiday time. I had completely lost the plot though. I was tired of darts, I was burnt-out. There had been a lot of problems. Sponsors who dropped out, not to mention the fact that my wife could barely move for 2 ? months. She had a back operation and was recovering on a hospital bed in our living room. Naturally I wanted to be with her and my family.

But I am not in a position where I can just put the brakes on and stop. If I had earned enough to be financially independent, I would most definitely have stopped for good. My dreams had almost all come true by then. Except one: To be the best dart player in the world. That will most probably never happen so I will have to make peace with that dream, however difficult that is for me. I find it hard to talk about this subject but I have to be honest. It's a fact so far and I have to learn to live with it. If I ever felt that my playing skills were deteriorating I would call it a day. On the other hand I know now that I can beat Phil Taylor. I have proved it and I should be able to do it again. I'm sure that I can still become world champion at least five times. But there you go, I want everything and that's not realistic, is it?

Apart from that, I have always wanted to be an ambassador for my sport. To promote it, and turn it into a world sport. I believe that I have taken the first step and succeeded in The Netherlands with this intention. If ever I put the arrows back in my top pocket for the last time and end my career, I would like to contribute to building and developing the sport of darts on a worldwide scale. At this moment in time this dream is probably still a long way off. I still love playing darts too much to want to stop at present. I'm still curious to find out how much more I can still achieve and if I can master areas of the sport that I still have difficulty coping with. For instance, I still don't like being in the spotlight. My main choice was to become a world champion dart player, not to be a famous Dutchman. That gets to me sometimes and it's a lot more difficult than many people imagine. Raymond van Barneveld is no longer Raymond van Barneveld. I have become Barney. I am recognised everywhere I go. Not only in Europe, but in many other countries as well. This is why I enjoy being by myself, withdrawing into my personal world. Why I wonder does no one understand that?

"I have seen his entire darts career unfold from close quarters", **Helen Hofland**, former director of the Dutch Darts League reflects. "At the start he was a skinny and difficult young man. He couldn't handle defeat or disappointments very well at all. Just as he reached the top of the Dutch rankings, he managed to fracture his playing wrist. That proved a terribly difficult time for him. He was extremely upset that he couldn't play for a while. What I saw in him then is what I continued to see for many years after. He was always battling with himself, and the people around him. Until he changed over to the PDC. That was the best decision he ever made in his life. Apart from marrying Silvia and becoming a father of three children, that is. He seems at peace with himself now. He is highly respected at the PDC and that is something he needs very much. The same goes for recognition. He has grown into a strong all-round player in the last few years. He doesn't need lucky dolls and chains any more. Just look at the 2007 PDC-final. How he recovered from being 0-3 down. In the past he would not have been able to make his way back from that point. In the old days his head would have quickly bowed down, because he couldn't handle defeat properly. It's because he's a very emotional person and so if he lost he would be ashamed. He's beaten that now and being able to fight back has made him more relaxed. You can see the change clearly when you compare his two major defeats to Jelle Klaasen. At the 2006 Lakeside he was not even placed. He couldn't handle that at all and he was totally unapproachable, to anyone! However, at the World Darts Trophy in 2007 he could, after only five minutes, put into perspective what had happened and why. In the past this would have been impossible. He has grown enormously as a person and as a sportsman.

The Dutch Darts League has also grown. A growth that is mainly down to him. When he played his first Embassy final in 1995 we only had 8,000 members. Three years later when he managed to win that same tournament for the first time there were 12,000 and now at present there are around 44,000. That's an incredible growth pattern for any sport. Mostly thanks to Raymond van Barneveld."

Of course not everyone hates me, I know that. But at the end of the day I always seem to be a figure of controversy. Whether people like me or not. 'He is still an icon, he pulled it off and is still doing it', I hear people say. It still hurts me a lot to think that sometimes, in The Netherlands, I'm being portrayed as arrogant. Most people don't really know me at all. Why do they judge me like that? I can't believe that when The Netherlands play England, the Dutch would support the English over the Dutch. That can't happen, can it? It happened to me though. The Dutch versus me. Unbelievable. People think I am a bit stuck up. But how can I change that? By not being myself, by acting? Always having a smile on my face? Sorry, I am a dart player, not a clown. It's ingrained in my character, and it is fed by this ever-returning lack of self-confidence. I've stopped demonstrating my victory gesture now: The one with clenched fists, leaning back and looking skywards. A lot of people found that arrogant or said that it didn't suit me. I can't even remember just how often I've been criticised for this way of celebrating. For some reason I'm someone who remembers the down side of life and easily brushes over the good times. But I do enjoy the good times as they occur. Over and over again. At the end of the day that's what makes all the difference. I hope."

International Titels

2007

Players Championship Las Vegas
Masters of Darts
Players Championship Duitsland
Las Vegas Desert Classic
Blue Square UK Open
Stan James Players Championship (Gibraltar)
UK Open North-East Regional Final
Ladbrokes.com World Championship

2006

Budweiser UK Open
Budweiser UK Open Midlands Regional Final
PDPA Players Championship Isle of Wight
Budweiser UK Open Irish Regional Final
Budweiser Scottish UK Open Regional Final
9-dart finish op Premier League Darts in Bournemouth

2005

Lakeside World Professional Darts Champion
Winmau World Masters
Couples World Champion WDF
Wereldkampioen over all WDF
Pacific Masters

2004

Bavaria World Darts Trophy
International Darts League
Doeland Grand Masters
Europees kampioen, singels, doubles and over all
Dutch Open
Finnish Open
Northern Ireland Open

2003

Bavaria World Darts Trophy
International Darts League
Doeland Grand Masters
Wereldkampioen WDF-
Embassy World Professional Darts Champion
Nine-Dart Finish at the Swiss Open

2002

Spring cup
IDPA Masters
Fantastika Masters
Open Zweden
Nine-Dart at the European Cup in Belgium

2001

Winmau World Masters
Spring cup
Dutch Open
Doeland Grand Masters

2000

Spring cup

European doubles champion

Swiss Open

1999

Embassy World Professional Darts Champion

World Champion WDF

Spring cup

Brandstaff Masters

The Belgian Open

1998

Embassy World Professional Darts Champion

Canadian Open

Swedish Open

British Open

1997

World Champion WDF

Norwegian Open

Danish Open

1996

The Belgian Open

1995

European Grand Masters

Finnish Open

1991

Spring cup

Distinctions

2006	Most popular player of 2006 (Poll Planetdarts.tv)
	Best newcomer (PDC)
2004	The Hague – The Public's prize
2003	IDPA Leighton Rees Men's Player of the Year Award
1999	The Hague – Haaglanden Sports prize
	Honorary citizen of The Hague
	Knight of the Order of Oranje Nassau
1998	The Hague – Sports prize
	The Hague – Haaglanden Sports prize
	BDO Personality Award
1997	The Hague – Sports prize

About the authors

Arnout Verzijl (1970) grew up in a village named Voorschoten, close to The Hague. After graduating successfully from the Regional Gymnasium high school in Leiden, he went on to study Social Sciences at the Erasmus University in Rotterdam. Mid way through the nineties he began his first job in journalism, working for the Dutch monthly football magazine *Voetbal2000*. During the years that followed he developed into an all round journalist/writer. In 1999 he made his debut as a reporter for *Nieuwe Revu* magazine covering *The Embassy*, the unofficial WC of darts. The coverage of EURO 2000 was his first big assignment as a football reporter. At present he works as Editor in Chief for *Elf Voetbal, a football magazine,* and *Darts International Magazine.*. He also was a correspondent for the press bureau Geassocieerde Pers Diensten (GPD). He has been published primarily in the daily Dutch papers *Trouw, Parool* and *NRC Handelsblad.*

It was in the spring of 1998 that he interviewed Raymond van Barneveld for the first time. Since then a warm and sincere friendship has developed that still continues to this day.

Hans Willink (1956) has worked for more than ten years as a sports journalist and photographer. During this period he has also worked in other areas. For instance, he has photographed almost every headline Dutch band, not to mention the Rolling Stones. He has also scribed a touristic piece about Rome for a family magazine.

Each month, together with a few colleagues, he works as a writer for the *Darts International Magazine*. Quarterly he writes for the *Nederland's Rugby Magazine* and once a year for a Beach volleyball magazine. He produces articles as well as images for these magazines.

In his journalistic capacity he worked amongst others for: The Dutch *NRC, Nieuwe Revu, Veronica Magazine, Spits, Elf* and *Sport International.* Willink first met Raymond van Barneveld in the early nineties. He interviewed him in a cafe in their hometown The Hague on behalf of the local radio station.

Since 1995 they have developed a very close bond, which became indestructible during the time that Verzijl and Willink followed Raymond around for nine days during the 1999 Embassy.